M. L Hurley

The Five Cardinal Principles of the Christian Church Defined

M. L Hurley

The Five Cardinal Principles of the Christian Church Defined

ISBN/EAN: 9783337003982

Printed in Europe, USA, Canada, Australia, Japan

Cover: Foto ©Lupo / pixelio.de

More available books at **www.hansebooks.com**

THE

Five Cardinal Principles

OF THE

CHRISTIAN CHURCH DEFINED.

EDITED WITH AN INTRODUCTION

BY

Rev. M. L. HURLEY,

CARRSVILLE, VA.

RALEIGH, N. C.:
CHRISTIAN BOARD OF PUBLICATION.
1886.
Presses of Edwards, Broughton & Co.

INTRODUCTORY.

Having for long years seen and felt the necessity of defining fully the cardinal principles of the Christian Church before the thinking minds of an intelligent public, I have at last determined to undertake the work. Its necessity may be seen in every local Church, and in almost every community.

Individuals studying the Cardinal Principles of the Christian Church are continually calling for explanations.

People of other religious organizations often ask such questions as—" Why do you assume the name *Christian?*"

"In appropriating that name to your denomination, do you not unchristianize all others?"

"Ought not all God's people to wear that name?"

This little volume proposes in a Christian spirit to answer these and like questions. Sometimes we are accused as a denomination, by friends and enemies, as having no test of church membership or church fellowship. We claim that Christian character or vital piety is the test of church membership, as a faithful perusal of these pages will show. The right of private judgment in matters of religion is often called in question, and oftener than otherwise is misunderstood.

The true position of the Christian Church upon the subject is fully defined. That definition is herein given. We have lost much by not defining fully our principles to the world. We have failed to give a reason for the principles that we hold. Consequently hundreds have, after conversion to God, sought homes in other religious organizations, because they did not fully comprehend our principles. Some say that we allow too much latitude, others say, not enough; hence the necessity for defining the true position of the Christian Church upon these leading principles.

In order that the work might not be considered as the voice or production of one man, but as the voice of the church, I have selected and secured the valuable services of five of the most pious and able ministers in the church to aid me in the preparation of this work. These brethren were selected from the church North and South, so that there is nothing of a sectional character in it. To strengthen this point, it has been endorsed by the General Convention of the Christian Church, the highest official body of the church in the Southern States.

Hoping that it may serve the end and fill the mission for which it was intended, it is cheerfully and respectfully submitted to the kind attention of an intelligent and thinking public.

M. L. HURLEY.

Carrsville, Va., July, 1886.

CONTENTS.

I.
THE LORD JESUS CHRIST IS THE ONLY HEAD OF THE CHURCH.
By Rev. James Maple, D. D., Raleigh, N. C.

II.
THE NAME CHRISTIAN.
By Rev. W. W. Staley, A. M., Suffolk, Va.

III.
THE SCRIPTURES OF THE OLD AND NEW TESTAMENT A SUFFICIENT RULE OF FAITH AND PRACTICE.
By Rev. J. P. Watson, Troy, Ohio.

IV.
CHRISTIAN CHARACTER THE TEST.
By Rev. J. W. Osborn, Ph. D., Swansea, Mass.

V.
PRIVATE JUDGMENT, THE RIGHT AND DUTY DUTY OF EVERY BELIEVER.
Sermon by Prof. Martyn Summerbell, M. A., of New York City.

THE FIVE CARDINAL PRINCIPLES

OF THE

Christian Church Defined.

I

CHRIST THE HEAD OF THE CHURCH.

By Rev. James Maple, D. D., Raleigh, N. C.

Ages before Christ was born into the world the Father said of him, "Behold, I have given him for a witness to the people, a leader and commander to the people." Isa. 55:4. There we have a clear statement of one of the relations that Christ sustains to his church. It is represented under the symbol of an army, and he is its commander. All the rules and regulations for its government originate with him. He is its head. God "hath put all things under his feet, and given him to be the head over all things to the church." He has appointed him the supreme ruler in the church. The mediatorial kingdom of Christ is the gift of the Father as the recompense of his humiliation and suffering. Paul states this connection clearly in the following passage, which at the same time gives us a sublime view of the exalted state of the Redeemer, and shows the unlimited extent of his dominions:—Let this mind be in you, which was also in Christ Jesus: who, being in the form of God, thought it not robbery to be equal with God: but made himself of no reputation, and took upon him the form of a servant, and was made in the likeness of men: and being found in fashion as a man, he humbled himself, and became obedient unto death, even the death of the cross. Wherefore God also hath highly exalted him, and given him a name which is above every name: that at the name of Jesus every knee should bow, of things in heaven, and things in earth; and things under the earth, and that every tongue should confess that Jesus Christ is Lord, to the glory of God the Father." Phil. 2:5—11. From this and other passages, we learn that nothing is exempt from his authority. He commands the armies of heaven; he claims the inhabitants of the earth as his subjects; he rules over the spirits of darkness; he is the Lord of the dead and the living. (Rom. 14:9.)

The proper object of Christ's mediatorial kingdom is the church, and our subject embraces his relation to it. It is the peculiar object of his care, and for the sake of it all power in heaven and earth was given unto him. By his personal ministry, and through the work of his apostles, he founded the church. The Christian Church is the work of Christ. He established it. He said to Peter "Thou art Peter, and upon this rock *I will build my church.*" Matt. 16:18. For this reason it is called the Son of man's kingdom. "The Son of man shall send forth his angels, and they shall gather out of his kingdom all things that offend, and them which do iniquity." Matt. 13:41. It is also Christ's household. (Matt. 10:25.) The members of the church are given to Christ by the Father out of the world, and are sent by him into the world. "Thou hast given him power over all flesh, that he should give eternal life to as many as thou hast given him." John 17:2. "Father, I will that they also, whom thou hast given me, be with me where I am." John 17:24. Christ is the head of the church, because he built it on the Rock of his Divinity, out of members given him by the Father out of the world.

The word head has several significations in the scriptures, besides its natural one, which denotes the head of man. It is sometimes used in the Bible to signify the whole man: "Blessings are upon the head of the just," Prov. 10:6; that is, upon their persons. God says of the wicked, "I will recompense their way upon their head." Ezek. 9:10. It sometimes signifies a chief or capital city: "The head of Syria is Damascus." Isa. 7:8. It denotes a chief or principal member of society: "The Lord will cut off from Israel head and tail." "The ancient and honourable, he is the head." Isa. 9:14, 15. Head also means one who hath rule and pre-eminence over others. Thus God is the head of Christ; as mediator, he receives all his dignity and authority from him. Christ is the spiritual head of the church, both in respect to eminence, power, and influence; for he communicates life, strength, knowledge, and influence to every believer. Paul says, "But I would have you to know, that the head of every man is Christ." 1 Cor. 11:3. "The stone which the builders refused is become the head stone of the corner." Ps. 118:22. It was the first in the angle, whether it was disposed at the top of that angle to adorn and crown it, or at the bottom to support it. Thus Christ is the life, strength and beauty of the church.

As the supreme head of the church Christ established the ordinances to be observed in it. He has appointed but two ordinances—baptism and the sacred supper. The institution of the supper is described by Matthew 26:26—28. "Jesus took bread, and blessed it, and brake it, and gave it to the disciples, and said, Take, eat; this is my body. And he took the cup, and gave thanks, and gave it to them, saying, Drink ye all of it; for this is my blood of the new testament, which is shed for many for the remission of sins." "This do in remembrance of me." Just before his ascension to heaven he commissioned his disciples and sent them out "into all the world" to preach his gospel. "Go ye therefore, and teach all nations, baptizing them in the name of the Father, and of the

Son, and of the Holy Ghost." Matt. 28:19. These are the only ordinances that he authorizes in his church, and no man, or number of men, has any right to appoint others. The authority of Christ over the church is exclusive of the authority of man. Councils may assemble to consult about the best methods, and to form plans for the conversion of the world, and the promotion of the spiritual interest of the church; but they can neither increase nor diminish the ordinances of the Lord's house. Christ's authority is supreme, and man's duty is to obey. "Let us hear the conclusion of the whole matter; Fear God, and keep his commandments: for this is the whole duty of man. For God shall bring every work into judgment, with every secret thing, whether it be good, or whether it be evil. Eccl. 12:13, 14.

Christ is the supreme lawgiver in the church. Human legislation has no place in it. "One is your master, even Christ." Matt. 23:8. "He is thy Lord; and worship thou him." Ps. 45:11. He holds supreme authority over the consciences and lives of men. The duty of the church is to submit to his authority; and it is not done unless his word is received as the only rule of faith and practice, and every thing which is practiced in religion be exactly conformable to his commands. He spoke by divine authority. He said, "The words that I speak unto you I speak not of myself: but the Father that dwelleth in me, he doeth the works." John 14:10. It is by the words of Christ, that man is to be judged in the last day. "He that rejecteth me, said Christ, "and receiveth not my words, hath one that judgeth him: the word that I have spoken, the same shall judge him in the last day." John 12:48. The word of Christ is the supreme law of the church, and the rule of life. This law is perfect, and meets all the emergencies of life. "The law of the Lord is perfect, converting the soul." Ps. 19:7. "But be not ye called Rabbi: for one is your Master even Christ; and all ye are brethren." Matt. 23:8. Christ is "King of kings, and Lord of lords"; and his word is the supreme law of his kingdom. The citizens of his kingdom all stand on the same level. "All ye are brethren," and one has no right to lord it over another. "There is one body, and one Spirit, even as ye are called in one hope of your calling; one Lord, one faith, one baptism, one God and Father of all, who is above all, and through all, and in you all." Eph. 4:4—6.

The Christian owes allegiance to Christ *alone*, and is responsible to him *only* for his faith and conduct. No man nor number of men, has any right to come between his conscience and Christ, and say what he must believe and do in order to be saved. This is a matter of conscience between him and his Saviour, and every man must settle this matter for himself. Christ is the sovereign and the judge. He makes the laws of his kingdom, and sits in decision upon the character of his subjects. Hence Paul says, " Wherefore we labor, that, whether present or absent, we may be accepted of him. For we must all appear before the judgment seat of Christ; that every one may receive the things done in his body, according to that he hath done, whether it be good or bad." 2 Cor. 5:9, 10. The supremacy claimed by the Pope, is an invasion of the royal prerogative of Christ; and he has intruded himself into this office, and assumes the power to change the ordinances, repealing the laws of Christ, and extending his jurisdiction over the visible and the invisible world. He "exalteth himself above all that is called God," and is worshipped; and, as God, he "sitteth in the temple of God, showing himself that he is God." (2 Thess. 2:4.)

Christ is the supreme head of his church because he is the author of the spiritual life of all its members. Paul says he "is our life." Col. 3:4. He is "the way, the truth, and the life." John 14:6. "The first man Adam was made a living soul; the last Adam was made a quickening spirit." 1 Cor. 15:45. "For as the Father raiseth up the dead, and quickeneth them; even so the Son quickeneth whom he will." John 5:21. Christ has the power to impart life, and "by him were all things created, that are in heaven, and that are in earth." Col. 1:16. It is through him that sinners are quickened from moral death, and made spiritually alive. "For we are his workmanship, created in Christ Jesus unto good works." Eph. 2:10. Christ illustrates this beautifully when he says, "I am the vine, ye are the branches." John 15:5. As the branch receives its life and fruitfulness from the vine, so the Christian draws his spiritual life and fruitfulness from Christ. He is the source of spiritual life to the church. "In him was life; and the life was the light of men." John 1:4. Hence it is said, "He giveth life unto the world." John 6:33. He summed up the whole matter when he said, "I am the resurrection and the life." John 11:25. Hence he is called, "The Prince of life." Acts 3:15. Prince here is used in the sense of *author*, or *giver* of life. Christian life is not merely an imitation and following of Christ, but a living, constant union with him. "Abide in me," said Christ, "and I in you. As the branch cannot bear fruit of itself, except it abide in the vine; no more can ye, except ye abide in me." John 15:4. Such is the vital communion between Christ and his people, and this caused Paul to use such expressions as "fallen asleep in Christ" (1 Cor. 15:18.), "I knew a man in Christ." (2 Cor. 15:2.), "I speak the truth in Christ" (1 Tim. 2:7.), and many others. God sent his only begotten Son into the world, that we might live through him. (John 3:16.) Thus we see that Christ is the source of the spiritual life to his church, and therefore its head.

This truth is illustrated in his relation to the church as its light. "In him was life; and the life was the light of men." John 1:4. Light is the symbol of truth, and Christ is the light of the world in the sense that he is *the* great Teacher through whom the way of life and salvation is revealed to man. Hence he says, "I am come a light into the world, that whosoever believeth on me should not abide in darkness." John 12:46. "I am the light of the world: he that followeth me shall not walk in darkness, but shall have the light of life." John 8:12. As the one infallible source of spiritual truth Christ is called "*The truth.*" John 14:6. As the moon borrows her light from the sun, because, of herself, she has little or none at all, even so the church can have no light of herself, but doth receive her light from the Son of God. The promise is, "But unto you that fear my name shall the Sun of righteousness arise with healing in his wings; and ye shall go forth, and grow up as the calves of the stall." Mal. 4:2. The church is a school of divine philosophy of which Christ is the Head, and from him alone we are to learn the truth. Other teachers may assist us in attaining a knowledge of the truth, but he is the only infallible teacher; and his word settles all controversy. It is the end of strife. He has made no mistakes. He is not only "holy, harmless, undefiled, separate from sinners"; but is absolutely perfect in knowledge. "In whom are hid all the treasures of wisdom and knowledge." Col. 2:3.

All things are made subject to Christ that he may use them for the good of the church. God "hath put all things under his feet, and gave him to be head over all things to the church." Eph. 1:22. This was done in reference to the church, or for its benefit and welfare. The universe is put under the authority of Christ that he may make "all things" tributary to the interests of the church. All the forces of the physical universe are subject to Christ, and he makes them serve the church. The kings and rulers, kingdoms and nations of earth, are subject to his authority; and he has so controlled them that they have not been able to injure his church. The very means that they used to crush it he has made to contribute to its advancement and spiritual growth in the end. The angels in heaven are under his authority, and employed by him to minister to the wants of the "heirs of salvation." (Heb. 1:14.) The fallen angels are under his control, and he will not permit them to injure his church. "The gates of hell shall not prevail against it." Matt. 16:18.

What an empire is this! Heaven and earth—the church militant—the church triumphant—all the mighty forces of the physical universe—angels, saints and seraphs. At his command the sweeping storm and rolling billows were hushed, demons crouched in terror and the grave yielded its prey! "Upon his head are many crowns." He is made "Head over *all* things, to his church." Yes, over *all* things, from the smallest to the greatest. He holds the stars in his right hand, and preserves every star in its spiritual orbit. With such a Head the church is safe.

THE NAME CHRISTIAN TO THE EXCLUSION OF ALL PARTY OR SECTARIAN NAMES.

By Rev. W. W. Staley, A. M., Pastor of Christian church, Suffolk, Va.

God has only one church. "Upon this rock I will build my church." Math. 16:18. Christ is the *foundation* of this church, "For other foundation can no man lay than that is laid which is Jesus Christ." 1 Cor. 3:11. He is also the *head* of this church. "He is the head of the body, the church." Coll. 1:18. "Which is the head, *even* Christ." Eph. 4:15. The scriptures employ various figures to represent this church. It is spoken of as a *family*. "Of whom the whole family in heaven and earth is named." Eph. 3:15. As a *building*. "In whom all the building fitly framed together groweth unto a holy temple in the Lord." Eph. 2:21. Unity is a cardinal principle in the gospel church. It is a body with many members, a vine with many branches. But it is, in scripture language, always one church with Christ as foundation and head. Christ is, moreover, the *life* of the church. "In Him was life; and the life was the light of men." John 1 : 4. "For the bread of God is He which cometh down from heaven, and giveth life unto the world." John 6 : 33. As one life pervades the church, all believers are bound into one body in Christ. This *principle* will be admitted by all who accept the gospel. But the *interpretation* of this principle some may strain. The multiplicity of parts in the gospel church is not denied; but this multiplicity, in their true relations, never breaks the bond of unity that makes the church one. It rather, like the multitudinous waves of the ocean, makes it the one grand church of Christ. The great cables that hold great steamers to the wharf are made of thousands of small strands, but they are so worked and twisted together that they become *one* in holding the ship to the shore. The church of Christ is wrought into one grand union of strain and life to hold the world to God. Whatever weakens this interwoven unity jeopardizes the salvation of men. All other questions merge into the stream of fraternal love, through which the united heart of the gospel church flows out into the boundless ocean of God's love. If the churches were closer to each other, they would be closer to their God.

With the principles laid down and the spirit indicated above, the name worn by the Christian church is here explained or defined.

Names, as applied to religious organizations, are all derivatives. Their value must, therefore, be determined by the *root* from which they are derived. This principle seems to be fair. It is not enough that they grow into large significance and wide reputation among men, laying the foundation for historic periods, and embracing many within their pale. The name should carry with it the origin of this gospel church, and ever teach, in part, this salvation through Christ to the world. The name is a part of this church. All inheritance comes in part by reason of name. The children of God are "joint heirs with Christ." Rom. 8:17. Buddhists derive their name from Buddha who was born near the end of the sixth century *before* Christ. Mohammedans derive their name from Mohammed who was born toward the close of the sixth century *after* Christ. Roman Catholics derive their name from the historic fact, that about the fifth century the Bishops of Rome claimed to speak with supreme authority. Very early in the Christian church the word Catholic (*Gr. Katholikos*), universal, had been employed to denote the world-wide offer of salvation by Christ in contrast with the particularism of the Jews. Hence it came to be used by ecclesiastical writers to denote the church as the depository of the doctrine of universal salvation in contrast with heretical sects. Since the Roman bishops claimed to speak with supreme authority, the term Roman Catholic church has been used. Lutherans derive their name from Martin Luther, the great Reformer of the sixteenth century. Calvinists derive their name from John Calvin who was born at Noyon, in Picardy, July 10, 1509. Baptists derive their name from the views they hold respecting the ordinance of baptism. This denomination had its origin no doubt in the sixteenth century, when there was a great awakening of religious thought and feeling. Methodists derive their name from the system introduced at first into Wesleyan societies. Members of the University of Oxford gave

Wesley and his society the name of "Methodists," in allusion to the *Methodici*, a class of physicians at Rome who practiced only by theory. This name thus given a century and a half ago came at length to be worn with pride by this large and growing denomination. Other names might be mentioned and their derivation traced out, and those already given could be enlarged upon with profit. The length of this chapter forbids, however, anything more than enough to establish the principle on which the name Christian is founded. There is no purpose to depreciate grand old names of historic value, or denominations whose numbers and activity bless two hemispheres. The aim here is only to search out in a plain way the significance of names as applied to religious bodies, and to discover, if possible, whether there is only one true name embracing all that should be worn by the church, to the exclusion of all party or sectarian names. The references are based on historic testimony and serve to illustrate the thought which is here presented. These bodies are all proud of their respective names. Their names are significant and fully reveal their meaning.

They are true exponents of what they are intended to signify. There has grown up with these names not only historic greatness, but truest attachment, and tenderest affection. The good and the great have lived under their shadow, and died in their communion, and their graves are honored with marble shafts and bedecked with roses. Great theologies have grown up around their peculiar tenets and literature is full of their thoughts and their labors. If the sleeping dust of their martyrs could speak, a thousand tongues would make earth ring with their praises. This is all true; and the world is better, and richer, and happier, and grander for its being true. But for all that, none nor all of these names combined set forth clearly and fully the origin of christianity to men. None of them in itself shows the relation of the church to Christ. The only name that *can* do this is *Christian*. This name presents clearly to men the origin of religion in the gospel church, and the relation of the church to its head, even Christ, "of whom the whole family in heaven and earth is named." Eph. 3:15. Perhaps all will agree that this is the only name that can set forth these two relations, and yet they may deny that this is necessary or that it was so ordained of God. Reverence for old things should never prevent the reception of truth. The attention of the reader is, therefore, directed to this point: What is the use of a name, as applied to the people of God? The object of a name is to distinguish the church, or the people of God, from the world and not to distinguish them from each other. The names referred to above and all kindred names serve to distinguish religious societies from each other, more than to distinguish them from the world. They serve very well to distinguish denominations from each other, and sometimes to hold them apart in love and labors. The name should be such as to distinguish the people of God from the *world*, and to show their relation to *Christ*. In this paramount demand these names seem to be insufficient, tending rather to division and strife than to union and love. Paul seems to be speaking on this, when he says to the Corinthians: "For while one saith, I am of Paul; and another, I am of Apollos; are ye not carnal?" 1 Cor. 3:4. The apostles insisted that the disciples should be attached to Christ and not to them. "A man can receive nothing, except it be given him from heaven." John 3:27. Besides, if these names are the true ones for the church, then centuries rolled away before she was properly named. None of these names goes back to the time of Christ. Either the name makes no difference, or these denominations wear wrong names. The *right* to wear the name *Christian* turns on the above condition. Some religious teachers hold the two following positions:

1. That the name *Christian* is common to all denominations, and that no one body has a right to wear the name to the exclusion of others.

2. That this name is not of divine appointment.

They think that men have the right to choose a name for the society which they compose. They claim this as one of the rights of the church. In other words, they claim the right of all evangelical churches to adopt names expressive of their peculiar tenets and practices. They think that God has left this matter with the church. Those

who claim the right of the church to name
herself must deny that any name has been
given by divine authority. Consistency requires this. This they do. The logical con-
sequences of these principles are such as to
lead into difficulty, when compared with the
attitude of these men toward the *Christians*.
They hold that men have the right to name
the church, deny that any name is from
heaven, and then deny the Christians the
right to call themselves by that precious
name. Are not the rights of all men in matters of religion the same? If the right of
choice in the matter of name belongs to all
other denominations, it belongs also to those
who chose to call themselves *Christians*.
The ages in their cumulative stores of wisdom and liberty are as open unto them as
unto others. The same rights of personal
choice belong to them that belong to other
branches of the church. If God has *not*
given a name for His church, and men have
the *right* to choose a name, then those who
call themselves *Christians* have the *same
right* to do so, that others have to choose
the names they respectively wear. This conclusion is inevitable from the premises of

those who hold that the *Christians* have no right to this name, exclusive of all sect names. The *Christians* claim equality of rights in matters of religion, with all other denominations, but not superiority over them; and upon the principles which others have laid down they wear this one name, of right. If there was no other ground upon which to stand, the *Christians* would stand on an equality with all other evangelical denominations.

This name has the sanction of usage, history, and the scriptures.

Luther, in his celebrated Theses, uses the term *Christian* whenever he refers to the true children of God; and Tetzel, in his reply, begins every proposition recorded by D'aubigni with that name. This shows that this name was important in their view, and had in it a significance pregnant with value to the church. It is dominant in the minds of all who truly comprehend the gospel as taught by Christ. But in the minds of many it is kept like conscience, under restraint. Many keep conscience in subjection to public sentiment or custom, and do not allow this moral sense to exercise its rights. They do the same in matters of christian belief and thought. They allow purely *church* influences to smother their personal convictions in matters of religious thought. Such are not free. Now the gospel of Christ sets men free. It removes the darkness and reveals the truth that is to save men. It liberates the captive and sets the prisoner free. "If the Son therefore shall make you free, ye shall be free indeed." John 8:36 Bunyan calls his best character in his " Pilgrim's Progress," "Christian." Now Bunyan was a Baptist, and to have followed out his church affiliations he should have called his leading character "Baptist." But that would not answer his purpose. It would have circumscribed the usefulness of his great book. It would have robbed the book of its universal appreciation, and limited its sphere of doing good. But he laid aside sectarian bias and gave the hero of this famous allegory that title which clearly sets forth to men the deep, settled view of his own heart as to name, and the world has accepted the work of his pen. In every gospel sermon where men plead with men to turn from their sins unto Cod, the appeal from all evangeical pulpits, is to become "Christians." The invitation to become a *christian* is invariably and without qualification made by gospel ministers in their appeals to the unconverted. It is only when men are urged to join the *church*, that denominational adjectives are used. Usage sanctions this name. It comes out like stars in the rifts of clouds, unconscious of itself, and revealing what is behind all sectarian titles. There is a common sense of things, all bathed in true religious life, that shows convictions covered by denominational restraints.

History sustains the claim to this name as the proper title for the church of Christ. Profane writers, who rank as standard authority, when they refer to the history of the gospel church, call it the Christian church. Josephus, Ant. 18:3—§3, employs this language: "Now, there was about this time (A. D. 33) Jesus, a wise man, if it be lawful to call Him a man, for He was a doer of wonderful works,—a teacher of such men as receive the truth with pleasure. He drew over to Him both many of the Jews, and many of the Gentiles. He was [the] Christ; and when Pilate, at the suggestion of the principal men amongst us, had condemned Him to the cross, those that loved Him at the first did not forsake Him, for He appeared to them alive again the third day, as the divine prophets had foretold these and ten thousand other wonderful things concerning Him; and the tribe of *Christians*, so named from Him, are not extinct at this day." As an example of profane historians I quote the first sentence in Gibbon's Decline and Fall of the Roman Empire: "In the second century of the *Christian Era*, the empire of Rome comprehended the fairest part of the earth, and the most civilized portion of mankind." That is the idea that pervades the history of civilized nations of nineteen centuries. Christianity is the one religion that engages the attention of the historian and calls forth words of praise from most skeptical pens. Ecclesiastical history treats the subject as the history of the Christian church. There starts with Christ a new period in the history of the world, and it gathers strength as it comes on from Bethlehem, with the babe over whose birth the heavenly host sang "Glory to God" and *to* whom the wise men bowed and presented their gifts of gold, frankincense, and myrrh; on by Gethsemane, and Calvary, and Joseph's new tomb, and the ascension, down through the blood of martyrs and brotherly love to this present age. This history in its life and its blessing for the nations has had its power in this grand fact. Whatever divides this idea into fragments weakens the saving force of this new life. The church in its aggregate life and work ought to keep this one idea before the world. There is no saving influence outside of this. Take this out of any denomination and there would not be enough left to save one soul. But some might ask, "Why is it then that you, as a people, do not succeed better and save more souls?" The answer is plain. The large bodies around us are not in sympathy with us. They look upon us as the Jews did upon Christ. The Jews prevented Christ from doing what He might have done with their sympathy and prayers. The doctrine of Christ required the surrender of many forms of Jewish thought and practice. The position held by the *Christians* pleads for a surrender of sectarian names. Men are unwilling to recognize such a plea. But such a surrender involves the loss of no principle that has in it any gospel power or saving force. · If all denominational titles were surrendered, there would still remain the same fundamental doctrines of this religion, and the same demands of gospel life. All that would be lost in such a course would be wordly honor, and fame. It might be the great Hudson losing her identity in the Atlantic; but she would be all the purer for that. That is what all need to lose themselves in Christ. All thought, and love, and work of God's people should be for Christ and the salvation of souls. But with many gospel ministers they do more work for their church than for the head of the church. They refer all their labors, all their thoughts, all their efforts to this one aim of building up the interests of their church. God demands of us more than this.

This inquiry would be incomplete if it failed to refer this matter to the word of God. That is the source of all things to the church. It is a revelation of God's will to man. It is higher in authority than usage, or history, or the acutest moral sense. It is final as authority for man in all matters of faith and practice. This word seems to sanction the name *Christian*, and this accords with what has been written before. The comment of Matthew Henry on Ephesians 3:15, sustains this view: "The universal church has a dependence upon the Lord Jesus Christ; *of whom the whole family in heaven and earth is named.*" The Jews were wont to boast of Abraham as their father; but now Jews and Gentiles both are denominated from Christ; so some. While others understand it of the saints in heaven, who wear the crown of glory, and saints on earth, who are going on in the work of grace here. Both the one and the other make but one family, one household: and from Him they are named *Christians*, as they *really* are such; acknowledging their dependence upon, and their relation to, Christ." The prophet Isaiah, in chapter 43:7, in speaking of the church and the relation of her members to God Himself, says: "even every one that is called by My name." Dr. Adam Clark in his comments on Acts 11:26, says: "It is evident they had the name *Christian* from *Christ* their Master; as the Platonists and Pythagorians had their names from their masters Plato and Pythagaros. Now, as these had their names from those great masters, because they attended their teaching, and credited their doctrines; so the disciples were called *Christians*, because they took Christ for their teacher, crediting his doctrines, and following the *rule of life* laid down by him. We are told in first Peter this: "If any man suffer as a *Christian*, let him not be ashamed; but let him glorify God on this behalf." (1 Peter 4:16.) In the notes on Acts 11:26, by Jacobus, there is the following: "*Christians*. Now that Jews and Gentiles were to be gathered into one church and communion, it was ordered in God's providence, that the body of believers should receive *a new name*, not national, but universal, and equally good for all people and all times; where there is neither Greek nor Jew, circumcision nor uncircumcision," &c., (Col. 3:11.) The fact is here recorded that the Disciples (or followers of Christ,) were first called *Christians* here at Antioch, where the first Gentile church was established. This name could not have been assumed by themselves, because it is used only twice in the New Testament besides this, and in a way to imply that it was a term of reproach and for which they were called to suffer. (1 Peter 4:16. ch. 26:28.) Nor could it have been given to them by the Jews, for they would not thus have acknowledged the Messiahship of Jesus by applying the term Christ (or Messiah) to His disciples. It was doubtless given to them by the heathen as a suitable name for distinguishing this body who were more and more prominent as followers of Christ, and would naturally be known by a name that should signify their relation to Him. The term itself seems to be rather of Roman than Greek origin. Yet it was doubtless also by the Divine ordainment that this should come to be their name, and the word signifying *called*, elsewhere means *called* by God, or by Divine direction. (Math 2 ; 12, 22; ch. 10:22; Heb. 8:5 ; 11:7.) This was more than ten years after Christ left the earth. They accepted this name, however reproachfully intended, and they gloried in it ; and often when threatened before magistrates their only answer was, "*I am a Christian.*" The church at Antioch was the first Gentile church. The gospel of Christ was to embrace all, both Jews and Gentiles. Perhaps this is why this name was not given when the first converts were made. The universal purpose of the gospel was to be settled before the church was named. God's purposes have often been carried forward by what was sin for men. The treatment Joseph received from his brethren was wrong, and yet the purpose of God was fulfilled in this man. "But as for you, ye thought evil against me; but God meant it unto good, to bring to pass, as it is this day, to save much people alive." (Gen. 50:20.) Judas sinned in betraying his master and yet it did not prevent the purpose of God. "But all this was done, that the Scriptures of the prophets might be fulfilled." (Matt. 26:56.) Let it be granted, then, that this name was given by those who had no purpose of doing service for the church in Antioch, yet no doubt it resulted in the fulfillment of the Divine purpose concerning His church. When Paul made his defence before Agrippa a deep impression was made upon the king. Said he to Paul: "Almost thou persuadest me to be a *Christian*." And Paul replied: "I would to God, that not only thou, but all that hear me this day, were both almost and altogether such as I am, except these bonds." (Acts 26:28.) Agrippa felt the force of Paul's argument, and still he was unwilling to accept christianity. He could not deny and he would not accept. But this shows that he knew the term that distinguished God's people. The King felt it and used it and Paul indorsed it. This name has ever been the one despised of men. And yet it ever presses its claims upon honest hearts. It asserts its significance in all pulpit appeals, in gospel work, in the history of twenty centuries, and in the word of God. The gospel is to the nations life and peace. The *Christ* in His *official capacity* is all in all to the church. Through Him the family of God is saved. From Him the family of God is named. Around Him the elect shall gather and rejoice in their eternal home. Before Him they shall stand arrayed in robes of white. At His feet they shall cast their glittering crowns. They shall be like Him, for they shall see Him as He is. They shall reign with Him in heaven, and He will be the light thereof. It will be the same family in heaven that Christ has upon earth. There will be no change in their character or their name. All that men can hope, is to enter heaven as they leave the world. There is no work nor device in the grave. As the tree falls, so it must lie. Heaven is the final dwelling-place of the family of God. No man can come unto the Father, but by Christ. That name which relates the pardoned to Christ, teaches the world that Jesus *is* the Christ, distinguishes the people of God from the world, removes the obstacles in the way of brotherly love, makes all the good in religion grow out of its head, reveals the origin and end of religion to men, preserves the only name given among men whereby we must be saved, is the one most worthy as a title for the church. This name is not claimed as the property of one society; it is claimed that it is the name by which all should be called. The conclusion already reached prepares for one of two views:

1. That if a name has been given by Divine direction for God's church, then that is *Christian*. There is no other that has such claim to Divine authority.

2. That if God approves names chosen by

men, then a society of believers has the right to adopt this name of their own choice.

The name is claimed therefore by right under 2 and by divine authority under 1. All other names will be unworthy a place in heaven. This name, *Christian*, would be appropriate in that bright realm. When the sun, and moon, and stars shall fade out in obscurity, the Lamb of God will light the kingdom wherein dwell the redeemed—when names now luminous with a brightness that outshines the sun and stars shall fade away in the distance, and revolutions and historic changes shall bring in others in the centuries yet unborn, the name *Christian* will shine on with a steady and increasing brilliance that shows the shining way to God. Human hearts will cling to it, and human love will gather around it, and conscience will own it, and history will embalm it, and God will defend it, because it binds the church to Himself.

RULE OF FAITH AND PRACTICE.

The Scriptures of the Old and New Testaments a Sufficient Rule of Faith and Practice. By Rev. J. P. WATSON, Troy, Ohio.

The Church, like the world, was built by Jesus Christ. This Church, too, was built on Himself, for He declares "On this Rock will I build My Church." (Matt. 16:18.)

The Apostles, through the ability which inspiration afforded them, are the expounders and illustrators of the Church in its historic fact and its general, moral doctrine. Christ and the Apostles appealed to the Old Testament Scriptures as the law and testimony for the confirmation of what they taught and did. Following this rule, the Scriptures of the New Testament, the authority of which is largely established by the teachings of the Old Testament, should be and have been universally appealed to by the Church of Christ, for the confirmation of its teachings and practices.

Than the Holy Scriptures, no chart and no compass have been given the Church of our Lord, from heaven. That the Church

Rule of Faith and Practice. 45

needs other chart or compass, would be very difficult of proof.

And yet, in the face of this apparent truth, very many denominations, embracing very great multitudes of honorable and intelligent Christian scholars within them, virtually, and to our judgment emphatically, contend that alone and unsupplemented by human additions or expositions, summaries or declarations, the Scriptures *are not* a sufficient rule of faith and practice. While making this anomalous and astounding declaration, both by word of mouth and practical illustration, they hold forth to us a little book, denominated a creed, discipline, or articles of faith, saying, ".this book *is* a sufficient rule of faith and practice." Of course they would not say, "This alone, without the Scriptures, is sufficient." But if we grant them this benefit, they cannot honestly and will not boldly affirm, if their action in formulating the creed means anything, that, "The Scriptures *alone* are sufficient." At best, their position is, "The Scriptures alone, as prepared by Jesus and his Apostles, are *insufficient*, but with the addition or association of the human and uninspired creed, they become sufficient."

This is most wonderful honor for the creed, but who can fail to see that the declaration and action are wonderfully dishonoring to the Scriptures?

By this action, for aught we can see to the contrary, the creed, as a rule and guide in faith and practice, is elevated above and pronounced superior to the Holy Scriptures, that law and testimony of heaven. By this action, the Scriptures are not simply relegated to a *second* place by *all* the creeds, but their inferiority or secondary importance, is proclaimed by *each* of the creeds.

The devotees of no one creed will say of any other creed than their own, "it comes nearer to the Bible than our own." The most exalted rank is held by each, in the estimation of its particular devotees, so that the Scriptures occupy at best, *the lowest rank* as a rule and guide. There are more than two hundred creeds extant, as the professions of as many divisions of the general Church and the Scriptures are pronounced inferior to *each and all* of them. If any *one* creed is admitted to be better than the Scriptures alone, who shall say that *each of all* is not?

Admitting the wisdom and correctness of our creed-friends, we are forced to the conclusion, that, while Prophets and Apostles, supplemented in their endeavors by the present and inimitable Christ, all failed miserably in formulating a sufficient rule and guide in faith and practice—the very end apparently, which they sought to attain. Any and every uninspired conclave of feeble men have proceeded with ease and accomplished this work with facility.

Although immensely in the minority and confessedly inferior in scholarship, the Christians are forced to take issue with this position and conclusion.

In this discussion we shall seek to show:

1. *That the* CREED *as a rule and guide* IS INSUFFICIENT.

2. *That the* SCRIPTURES *as such a rule and guide* ARE SUFFICIENT.

The insufficiency of the creed is shown,

I. *By the number of them extant.*

They who formed the second creed proclaimed thereby the insufficiency of the first, while each subsequent formation was a proclamation of the insufficiency of the preceding.

Surely no one is so well qualified to speak of the insufficiency of the creed as those who have tried them, and if by the process of the new formations all preceding formations are pronounced insufficient, it would be presumption to ask implicit faith and confidence in the new and untried one.

Great Britain boasts of 150 varieties of Protestantism, each one of which has a creed differing from all others. No one body of these people thought the Scriptures an adequate rule and guide, and no one feels that the creed of either other body would prove adequate to their wants. Here we find universal rejection and condemnation of the *other man's creed*, which amounts with all to a rejection and repudiation of *all* the creeds. This looks like a pretty strong verdict against the creed as a whole, even by that innumerable multitude which insists on our adopting the creed.

Presbyterianism can boast of 50 distinct divisions under its name, and at their Ecumenical Council, held in Philadelphia in 1883,

Rule of Faith and Practice.

thirty-two of these divisions were represented.

Each division of this many-headed people feels that its creed (for each is supplied with a separate creed), is a rule and guide sufficient; but they share not this feeling with reference to the creed of either other division.

Moreover, the very wise and sufficient creeds of this shamefully divided body of Christians were so unlike and antagonistic indeed, that during that general convention not once was the name of Jesus heard in song, nor could they agree to celebrate together the sufferings and death of their Lord and Master at the Communion table. Is not the sufficiency of the creed best seen, after all, in leading the brotherhood both away from Christ and from each other? If the creed does not, better than the simple Scriptures, lead the soul *to* Christ and bind the heart of brother *to* brother, wherein shall we see its superiority as a rule to the Scriptures, or its *sufficiency* in any respect? Instead of being a means of union, the creed has proven itself a wall of separation, and if, as a rule, it is sufficient in faith and practice, the faith to which it conducts is hardly that of Christ (else Christ has many faiths), nor its practice that of brotherly love and Christian courtesy.

That the creed is *insufficient* is further seen :

II. *In the badness of the spirit to which it leads.*

We would not say that the phraseology or spirit of the creed is malicious, but history and the opinions of eminent men are both at fault, if the creed does not lead to and beget an unbrotherly, oppressive and vindictive spirit. If it diminishes brotherliness, or in the least fosters and feeds the passions and flames of condemnation and persecution, then its value for good has been overstated, and its repudiation as a moral agency in the hands of Christian men cannot be too emphatic.

In City Hall, New York City, Jan. 30, 1876, the Rev. James Poindexter affirmed that not less than 70,000,000 of men had been slaughtered in the name of Christ in the effort to make them subscribe to, and observe, religious creeds. If this is truthful, or if the 70th part of it be true, then I submit a second to the motion of another, that the creed be bound in *red*. Accepting the minimum amount of the truth of this assertion, what a fearful commentary is it on both the *insufficiency* and the absolute *evil* of the creed as a moral influence and agent. "It has been said," remarks Dr. Beaumont; "that not less than 50,000,000 Protestants, at different times, have been put to death by Papists. What an army! What seas of blood have been shed! If their bodies were piled in one heap, that heap would be bigger than any mountain in the world." If these 50,000,000 had subscribed to the Papal creed, how many of them would have perished? If subscription to the creed of Rome would have saved their lives, as beyond reasonable question it would have done, did not the non-subscription of it cost them their lives? In other words, was not the creed, or the spirit which it inspired in its devotees, responsible for the slaughter of these millions? If Rome had no creed but the Bible, yielding to each the privilege of the personal interpretation thereof, would those persecutions unto death have transpired? The answer must be a negative one, and thus illustrates the vengeance of that spirit awakened by the creed.

Between 1553 and 1558 Queen Mary led more than 200 chiefs of the Protestant party to the stake in England. Would either one of these chiefs have perished if he had renounced his own and embraced the creed of Mary's Church? How inexorable is the spirit of the creed, and what torches it has lighted to illumine its way of progress in the earth! Discarding the light of the Word, it has led its followers by the light of fagot across many nations and around the world.

While the spirit of Protestantism is less severe, because more enlightened, it has, nevertheless, made an altar of its creed innumerable times, whereon it has castigated and slaughtered myriads of protesting victims.

The word persecution, as used by different denominations between themselves, which the light of history in smallest measure only too painfully reveals as a fact, would have been sheathed by the surrender of one creed and the adoption of another, or better yet, by the surrender of all creeds and the adoption of the Bible alone.

That the *creed* as a rule is *insufficient*, appears:

III. *In that it discourages free thought and important investigation.*

It is a form of infallibility. The *people* may change but the *creed* never does. If the people are not satisfied with the *old* creed they are at liberty to form a *new* one. The mind and heart will open, but the iron ribs of the creed will not stretch, and he who would have more liberty must seek a larger house. Infallibility is the voice of the creed, whether Protestant or Catholic, and it is quite as honorable and admissible in the one as in the other. A great hue and cry is made over the Pope's assumption of infallibility, but the work of every Protestant council that ever formulated a creed has been marked *infallible* as well. The creed may possibly manifest some measure of thought, but it most certainly discourages, if it does not absolutely forbid, *further* thought. The council, they say, went prayerfully to the Bible for their creed, but they are utterly unwilling that any others should, and if they persist in doing so, excommunication is the penalty. The nobler mind *will* think and formulate its own faith, but if it does, and persists in proclaiming it to the world, the loss of church-fellowship must result.

If the creed lessened free thought only with reference to human speculations, it would not be so bad, but it does more and worse, by far.

If it does not turn the mind away from the Bible, it begets within the man the old Catholic conviction, that he cannot understand it of himself.

Why should he, for his doctrine, study the Book, when he may not understand it and which it took a council of wisest theologians to expound? If it does not turn a man from the Word, he will approach it with his mind warped and narrowed by stereotyped opinions. He will accept from the Word only such truths as his creed approves, and his creed becomes thus the key of the Word's interpretation. In the light of this argument, we cannot see but the creed is a bar to free investigation and enlarged moral intelligence! Free Bible study will not lead to uniformity of doctrinal belief. The creed is intended to do this, and to a large extent it will. Thus its spirit is unlike that of the

Word and antagonistic to it. It enervates the mind by thinking for it, or relieving it from the responsibility of thought and is thus antagonistic to human progress.

The creed is *insufficient*, in that—

IV. *It leads to an untruthful expression.*

"An honest man is the noblest work of God," one has said. No one will question that the Bible leads to honesty of expression. We are emphatically of the opinion that *the unyielding creed does not and cannot lead to, or suffer honesty, in the heart's expression.* Whenever the creed-church is true to itself, and thus honest in its own action, *it will require a personal endorsement of its creed by the member it receives to its fellowship.* That it ever deviates from this rule, does not prove its liberality, but *its absolute dishonesty*, and beside, in receiving a member who disbelieves its creed, as it often will, *it winks at and encourages a dishonest expression in that member.*

Both of the above acts would be dishonorable in simply a *moral* man, or in a merely *moral* institution. Nine times in ten, the member to be received will consent to the truth of the creed, before the church or the examining board, even if he does not understand the meaning of the creed, or if, in understanding, he disbelieves it in whole or in part. In a majority of cases, the creed is not understood, and in a majority of the balance, it is not literally believed. For a church to accept the assent of the mind to an uncomprehended statement, is *shameful*, and for it to accept such affirmation when untruthful, is little better than *wickedness.* When a place within the church is at the price of honor and manhood, it is too dearly won, and when the church is ready to reject the man who honestly differs from a certain creed, while accepting the Bible as a fact from God, it certainly is not worthy to call itself the Fold of Jesus or the Church of Christ. That the creed, while professed, is not an honest expression with a large portion of the *laity*, has illustration in a statement of " *The Methodist*," a newspaper of New York city, in 1878. It says: "We have discovered 1,000 families in Brooklyn, that have left the M. E. Church for other denominations, and 980 of these families assigned as the reason of their departure the changeableness of the pastorate." Now, these families turned away from the creed of Methodism, which was their avowed doctrinal belief, and embraced another and contradictory creed, without any change in their *doctrinal* convictions. If they were *honest* in saying "the Methodist creed is our belief," they were *not honest* in adopting the antagonistic creed of another denomination. But as with the laity, so is it with the *clergy*. In 1878 there were 500 applications on file with the Bishops of the Reformed Episcopal denomination, from clergymen of other denominations, for positions in their ministry. These gentlemen would all doubtless continue to represent the doctrinal faith of their respective denominations, until they could, with financial safety, pass over to the arena of a new and another faith.

It may be said that the difference between the creeds of the different denominations is so slight, that layman or minister can pass over from one to the other, even without change of belief and without any compromise of honor or honesty. But this is not the truth. If the differences of creeds are so slight and unreal, why may not union be effected through minutest compromises and concessions. The differences of the creeds are sharp and radical, and such a thing as dovetailing one into the other is wholly impossible. The creeds will not blend, but the hearts of the people would do so were it not for the creeds.

Whenever a ministerial defection occurs, the press of the suffering body proclaims a change of faith, the which, if sincere, unfits the man for remaining and makes his departure both necessary and desirable. Do the different denominations proclaim the indistinctness and littleness of their dividing lines and assure their ministers and members that they can consistently and easily pass over into the embrace of other denominations? They ought to know if the differences are so slight. Would to God they would so talk, and the dividing lines, for a fact, would soon disappear. Radical differences are proclaimed as a fact, however, and these differences are magnified for effect. The separating creedal walls are without *open gates* from one camp into another, nor are those walls as low as some imagine.

V. *The Holy Scriptures are a sufficient rule of faith and practice.*

Rule of Faith and Practice.

We thus conclude,

1. *From their inspiration.*

This, certainly, is a very essential element of the word, and the grandest claim that can be made for it. Such a claim will be made, probably, for no creed extant, and if there is any value in inspiration, then, by so much as this, at least, is the Bible better than the creed. Of their inspiration, let the Scriptures speak for themselves.

Paul says, "All Scripture is given by inspiration of God." (2 Tim. 3 : 16.) Peter says, "This Scripture must needs have been fulfilled, which the Holy Ghost spake by the mouth of David." (Acts 1 : 16.) And David for himself, says, "The Spirit of the Lord spake by me, and His word was in my tongue," (2 Sam. 23:2.) Paul confirms David's testimony of himself, (Ps. 95:7,) by saying, "Wherefore, the Holy Ghost saith to-day if ye will hear His voice harden not your heart." (Heb. 3:7.) Peter says, "For the prophecy came not in olden time by the will of man, but holy men of God spake as they were moved upon by the Holy Ghost." (2 Peter 1:21.) These declarations cover the inspiration of both the Old and New Testaments, which, together, constitute the Christian's rule of faith and practice. By consent of all, the creed is without inspiration or divine authority. The Scriptures, on the testimony of David, Peter, Paul and Jesus, come to us enstamped and sealed with both. We say, "Our rule and guide are sufficient because *inspired.*" The creed-devotees say, "Our rule and guide are more nearly sufficient, although *uninspired.*"

The sufficiency of the Scriptures further appears:

2. *In that which the Sacred Writers claimed them to be.*

David says, "Thy word is a *lamp* unto my feet and a *light* unto my path." (Ps. —) Solomon says, "For the *commandment* is a *lamp* and the *law* is a *light.*" (Prov. 6:23.) David further says, "O send out Thy *light* and Thy *truth:* let them lead me; let them bring me unto Thy holy hill, and to Thy tabernacles." (Ps. 43:3.) Jesus tells us what David's "*truth*" is: "Thy *word* is *truth.*" (John. 17:17.) Hear David further, "The *law* of the Lord is *perfect, converting* the *soul.*" (Ps. 19:7.)

Surely, for a traveller over a road untrodden and in a way often dark, nothing could prove more valuable than a *light* and a *lamp*. The perfection of the Scriptures as an *illuming* agency, both for the heart, the way of life and the cradle of final rest, even the creed-monger and lover will not contend against. It would be like audacity, however, for a Christian to say, " My *creed* is a *lamp* unto my *feet* and a *light* unto my *path*." Then, more can be said for the *Bible* than the *creed*. David sought for no creed as a guide and rule in faith and practice, and who will say that beside the Scriptures he needed any? Is the way darker before us, or more difficult than before David, that we need more light than he had! It is not darker, nor more difficult, and yet, with the New Testament added to the Old, we have more than double his light. Strange that we should not be content with this! He was willing to be led by the Holy Scriptures, and they did lead him to rest, security, devotion and salvation. Can the creed lead to more than these? What they did for David they would do for any other person, and securing what David did, what can we want beside? If the Scriptures are " perfect, converting the soul," will they be more than perfect, or do more than convert the soul, or indeed more easily convert the soul, with the creed added? By the voice of the Old Testament the Scriptures are a perfect *lamp, light, law, commandment, guide* and *converting agency.* What more could we wish them to be, and what can be more? The creed cannot be so much; therefore the *creed is a less perfect rule and guide than the Bible.* But open the New Testament and listen to Jesus: "Search the Scriptures; for in them ye think ye have eternal life: and they are they which testify of Me." (John 5:39.)

If the Scriptures give eternal life and reveal Jesus to the soul, do they not, in these two particulars, do more than the creed? Can we want more than Jesus and eternal life? And who will say that we cannot have them without the creed? If the Scriptures alone lead to Jesus and give eternal life, then, *thus far*, they must be a sufficient and perfect rule of faith and practice. Where is the wisdom or right in substituting the creed for them? What man will venture to apply the above quotation to the creed? Hear Paul: "Thou hast known the Holy

Scriptures, which are able to make thee wise unto salvation through faith which is in Christ Jesus. All Scripture is given by inspiration of God, and is profitable for doctrine, for reproof, for correction, for instruction in righteousness: that the man of God may be perfect, thoroughly furnished unto all good works." (2 Tim. 3:15-17.) What a wonderful statement is the above, and who would seek its modification! Here, the simple Scriptures, without the help of the creed, make the man wise unto salvation, perfects him in character, and fully furnishes him in good works. Have they not proven their sufficiency in these three directions? Has the creed proven *its* sufficiency in either one of these directions, or can it do so? If it has not and cannot, why boast of its superiority or sufficiency? The very things the Scriptures do for the man he needs to have done for him, and if they will not do this work better with the creed than without it, then the creed is not needed to make him wise unto salvation, perfect him in character or qualify him for good works. Is the creed a better *instructor, reprover, corrector,* or *indoctrinator* than the Bible, or is it as good?

If not, then in *seven particulars*, just•here, it is far short of, and less helpful, than the Scriptures. It would be difficult to indicate *one* desirable thing in which the *creed* is better than the *Scriptures alone*, or the tithe as good, or one thing wherein the creed makes the Scriptures more perfect as an agency. What good use the creed can serve, or for what *one* thing it is a sufficient guide in faith and practice, I fail to see or know. If it will do for the man *one thing* which the Bible alone cannot do—one thing which the man, to the perfection of his character and his moral effectiveness needs to have done, then I should yield it some little measure of respect. Until then, I can only loathe it for its false claims and evil fruits.

We will see Scripture sufficiency further, in that,

3. *They were the only rule of faith and practice with the Primitive Church.*

As with the primitive *Christian* Church, so was it also with the *Jewish* Church: "They have Moses and the Prophets; let them hear them." (Luke 16:29.) God gave the Jews the Old Testament for a guide, and *they* were content. To the Old, he has added the New

Testament as a guide for the Christian Church, but *they* are not content To these Old Scriptures the Bereans appealed (to no creed), for "they searched the Scriptures daily, whether those things were so." (Acts 17:11.) It would be difficult to prove that Moses, Jesus, Peter, Paul, John or James, ever appealed to any other standard than the Scriptures as a rule and guide in moral faith and practice. If the creed can show a better rule for the government of *conduct* than Jesus gave in Matthew 18:15—17, then we will admit that it possesses a virtue heretofore undiscovered by us. As to what constituted the rule of *faith* with the Apostles, we refer the reader to the Pentecostal occasion and to the personal cases of the Eunuch, Cornelius, Lydia, the Jailor and Saul. Surely these disciples and the early churches to which they belonged were not left without a sufficient rule of faith and practice, and yet who will claim that they were supplied with any form of creed, or any rule whatever, save the teachings of the sacred New and Old Testament writers. The simple fact that the Scriptures were the only rule or guide in the Mosaic and Apostolic churches, and that no semblance of a creed is discoverable until about 100 years after the death of John, and that even those then formed were without binding authority according to most eminent authority, must go far to demonstrate both the sufficiency of the Scriptures, and that no other rule and guide was intended for the Church of Jesus.

The sufficiency of the Scriptures alone will appear:

4. *In their Moral or Regenerating Power.*

That the Bible is a *converting* agency has been affirmed by Paul to Timothy, and that *alone* it is such an agency, and thus sufficient as a guide to regeneration, will appear from a few illustrations following: In Rio Novo, Brazil, a man obtained a copy of the Bible, which he read to his Catholic neighbors, and its spirit so touched their hearts that they sent to Brotas for a missionary. On his arrival he found 200 converts ready for church organization, and these conversions were the fruit of that one Bible alone.

Another instance: An East Indian, who had been a priest of Budhism for forty years, picked up a leaf from the Gospel of John, which so interested him that he sought and obtained a copy of the New Testament. After reading it, he said: "I will follow Jesus." He read it to his wife and children and they believed and bowed to Jesus. He then gathered the town people and read it to them, winning many of them to Christ. This all occurred before they had ever been visited by a missionary.

Again: In Japan, in 1860, a Bible was left in Souda by a traveller. Not until 1875 was the place visited by a missionary, and then, as the fruit of that Bible, he found a band of Christians ready for organization. *The Bible alone converted, saved, transformed* and *christianized* these people. Whoever heard of such a work resulting from the creed alone, or even of a single conversion through its instrumentality?"

During the Abysinian war a number of Bibles were left by the soldiers among the natives. They resulted in the conversion of 120 persons, among whom were 33 Mohammedan priests. They were driven out by the natives, and sought the protection of the British flag.

At Kooz Oglook, an Armenian village, the Rev. Mr. Goss, on a visitation, was ill-treated and finally driven away. He left behind him a single copy of the Bible. Ten years later a second visitation was made, and it was found that 30 families had become Christians through the agency of that one Bible.

Even in Christian lands the Bible shows the same remarkable energy as a converting agency. Lord Lyttleton was converted from pronounced infidelity by reading the wonderful story of Saul's conversion. Finney, the distinguished revivalist, is an illustration of the same truth. As an unconverted lawyer, he would not have a copy of the Bible about until finally, to perfect himself more fully for his professional duties, he purchased a copy, in order to acquaint himself with the Institutes of Moses. This study led to his conversion and the changing of his profession.

These illustrations amply manifest the moral efficiency of the Scriptures unaccompanied by the creed, and show conclusively that "the Sword of the Spirit, which is the Word of God," has an edge quite as keen as that claimed for it by the Apostle.

Rule of Faith and Practice. 69

The sufficiency of the Scriptures is shown further:

5. *In their universal adaptedness.*

There is not a nation known to us which cannot take the Bible into the folds of its heart and get therefrom the needed moral consolation, instruction and correction. As it was with the early Christians—Jews, Greeks and Romans—so is it yet to all men everywhere. As one has said : " The Bible is the only world-book "—and such it most truly is. It has been called "the Englishman's book," but is far more than this: "*It is man's book*" in the most universal sense.

Goethe remarked : " The Bible is not only a popular book, but it is the book of the peoples—the more the ages shall progress in culture, the more shall the Bible be used as the foundation and as an instrument of that education which forms truly wise men."

General Grant said recently : " To the influence of the Bible we are indebted for all the progress made in true civilization, and to this we must look as our guide in the future."

General Putnam once remarked: " The Bible is the most wonderful book I ever heard of. It has something for everybody and for all occasions."

Certainly all that is said here for the Bible, any creed-loving minister would endorse and emphasize, but what one of the above things can he say for his creed? Is the creed of Methodism, which is just as perfect as any creed, as fully adapted to the wants of the people morally as is the Bible! If they were told that they must give up their Bible or their creed, would they not, *ten thousand times over*, prefer to give up the latter? By yielding their creed they might cease to remain Methodists in some respects, but having the Bible left, would they therefore cease to remain Christians? As the Bible is dearer to them than their creed can be, so to remain Christians is infinitely better than to remain simply as Methodists. Dispossession of his creed would not unchristianize the man, but without his Bible he would soon lose sight of his Christ. Now the Bible, our Methodist friends would tell us, is perfectly adapted to their wants. But would not the Presbyterians, Baptists and Lutherans all tell us that the Bible is as perfectly adapted to their wants? Is either creed of these denominations as perfectly adapted to the wants of all the rest? And if all had to agree on any one creed, or the simple Bible, as their rule of faith and practice, would there be a moment's hesitation in the choice? Certainly not! Then, is not this decision to be accepted as a judgment by all in favor of the Scriptures alone over any other creed than their own creed? And as this judgment, of course, is a repudiation of each creed, does it not elevate the Bible as a rule and guide above all the creeds?

Now, then, all creed-denominations differ from the Christians *in just one particular. They each would prefer the Bible alone to any creed than their own, while the Christians would prefer the Bible alone to any creed whatever!* While the Christians say: "the Bible is a sufficient rule of faith and practice," the 200 or more creed-denominations say: "the Bible and our 200 creeds are a sufficient rule of faith and practice." Does either one denomination say of the creed of any other denomination, "*It* is a sufficient rule of faith and practice?" Does not each creed-denomination say to every other creed-denomination: "Your creed *is not* a sufficient rule and guide." *Then taking the testimony of all denominations, do we not find it fully confirmatory of the position of the Christian that no creed is a sufficient rule and guide in faith and practice?* We have not tried the creed, but while all creed-bodies virtually decide against the creed in its sufficiency, save as formulated by its own hand, would it be wisdom in us to turn from the Scriptures to the creed?

Bible sufficiency is further manifested in that:

6. *Most enlightened judgment pronounces in favor of this truth.*

Coleridge says: "The Bible is the only adequate organ of humanity. It has gone hand in hand with science, civilization and law." If the Bible will answer as "the organ of humanity," to which claim all denominations will consent, then is it not sufficient as the organ of a single denomination? Will that do for the whole which will not do for a part? All denominations together, in any capacity, will accept nothing else. This certainly is a warm and blessed verdict in favor of the grand old book. We would think that he who could command an immense army ought to have no trouble in commanding a small division of that army.

"The Bible, the whole Bible, and nothing but the Bible," was the motto of the Reformation. This, without modification, is the motto of the Christians. Whoever thought of challenging the wisdom of the Reformers in the adoption of this motto? Would to God they had been content to abide by it alone and forever! Are the Christians to be blamed, or are they not safe in adopting the motto of the Reformation? We have tried it for seventy-five years, and it has led us on to no rocks as yet. If the Protestant world will accept our invitation to try it with us, we will soon again be back in the palmy days of the Reformation. Chillingworth, the grandly eloquent minister of the Episcopal church, could go as far as the Christians have gone in at least his word-of-mouth proclamation. "The Bible—the Bible the religion of Protestants." He did not say, "the Bible and the creed," or "the Bible as interpreted by the creed," but "the Bible" (and nothing else) "the religion of Protestants." Does the creed add to the religion of the Bible, or make that religion any better? Is not the religion of the Bible in its faith and practice all-sufficiency? What more than this all-sufficiency can we have, or reasonably wish?

Lonza, Ex-Prime Minister of Victor Emanuel, of Italy, once remarked: "The Divine Book which proclaims the abolition of slavery, universal brotherhood, peace on earth, benevolence to the poor, etc., ought to have power to meet the utmost needs of the State, and to be the creed of our entire humanity." Thus eminent men unfurl the banner of the Scriptures inscribed "*The Organ of Humanity*," "*The Motto of the Reformation*," "*The Religion of Protestants*," and "*The Creed of Humanity*." Let any one of the creed-denominations unfurl such a banner over their own creed, and all the other creed-denominations would ridicule the act with a laugh of scorn! If the creed-denominations would unite in protestation against, and ridicule of, this assumption by *any one* of their creed-bound fellows, is it wisdom to pronounce the Christians unevangelical, when they really but imitate the *full* example of *all* in *their* denomination of such unwarrantable assumptions?

Finally, the sufficiency of the Scriptures appears in that:

7. *They will do more for the Church than the creed can and far more without the creed than with it.* For the creed, it is claimed that *it will assure soundness of faith, give plain expression to that faith, protect against dangerous elements* and *bind the people more closely together.* To be better than the Scriptures, it ought to do all of these things, and if it does do them then the creed should be substituted for the Scriptures as our *creed-denominations* insist.

If, however, the creed will do neither of these things as well as the Scriptures, then surely the Scriptures should be substituted for the creed, as a rule of faith and practice, as the *Christians* insist. Soundness of faith is very desirable and the *true faith* the Scriptures claim to set forth (and all creed-denominations admit that they do,) in the language which the Holy Ghost teacheth. Is not the Holy Ghost a safe and sound teacher? Have our creed-friends found a safer and sounder teacher or teachers in certain uninspired and erring men, that have met as councils, in different ages of the world? Do the *Armenians* say that these councils, when *Calvinistic*, have been sounder and safer than that council of the Apostles, with Christ as its Head? Will the *Calvinistic* friends say the same of *Armenian* councils? Will *Protestants* say the same of *Catholic* councils? or *Catholics* the same of *Protestant* councils? Each repudiating the authority, safety, soundness of the other, to whom shall we turn, that we *may* have soundness of faith? The Scriptures teach God's Fatherhood, man's brotherhood, Christ's Messiahship, the quickening and consoling power of the Holy Ghost, the necessity of resgeneration, baptism, the reurrection and the final judgment, together with the return of Jesus—as all admit. Do the creeds teach any more than these doctrines, or these doctrines in a sounder and safer form? If a man believes in these doctrines, is he not sound in the faith? and if he gets them first-handed from the Bible alone, is he not just as safe and sound in matters of faith as if he took them second-handed and in unscriptural language, from the creed? Who-

Rule of Faith and Practice. 77

ever accepts the Scriptures as his rule of faith, believes all these doctrines, and is, therefore, sound in the faith. Such a man does not need the creed, so that it is not true that the creed *assures soundness of faith.* Nor does the creed *more plainly illustrate* the man's faith than the Scriptures. "We cannot tell what you believe," the Christians are often told; therefore you should adopt a creed. Most ridiculous and yet most common, is this assertion. But we answer, "Can you not tell what Paul believed and John and Peter and James? Did they accommodate your squeamish notions by presenting you with a creed, wherein was condensed in some other than Scriptural language their peculiar doctrinal ideas? When we say, "We believe the teachings of Paul, John, James, Peter and Jesus, are we not as definite as they were?" And when you say "We cannot tell what you believe," when we make their word our belief, do you not charge these writers with indefiniteness and ambiguity? Affirm any one thing which the Bible, in its own language affirms, and in that very language we will give you our belief and teaching. Are you not unreasonable in demanding that we repudiate the plain, Bible teaching and adopt for your accommodation the ambiguous and unscriptural language of an uninspired and unauthorized creed? We appeal "to the law and to the testimony." We will not be driven from the Bible alone, for it is the only fortress behind which the soul is safe.

If 1,000 men arise and proclaim their belief in exactly the same language, and that language not Bible language, it would look as though they had learned their doctrines in the school of human masters, rather than in the school of Christ and his Apostles. We are asked, but we are not yet ready, to exchange the latter school for the former. If the creed gives such plain expression to Christian faith, why do they state that faith in 200 ways, no two of which are alike? Does Paul differ from James, or Peter from John? or either one from Christ? And yet, these men whom we are asked to follow, that we may *plainly* state our faith to the world, strangely disagree in their statements of faith? Thus the creed fails in two points, and in these its claims are manifestly false. But we are told, "*The creed will protect your Church against dangerous elements.* Shall we protect ourselves against Methodists, Baptists, Lutherans, Presbyterians? Are these dangerous elements for the church? Or is any man dangerous who loves God with all his heart and his neighbor as himself—who accepts Jesus as his Saviour and the Bible as God's Word to his soul?

It surely cannot be the *character* of the Christian which is an element of danger, against which we should guard, nor indeed his *faith*, if he draws it directly from Christ and his Apostles? We invite to our fellowship *Christian men*, because Christ himself has entered the throne of their hearts and would readily open the gates of heaven to them. Do the creed-denominations fill their churches with a better class of men than *Christians*, and find men robed with a better character than *Christian* character? Do they dare claim that, in point of character, their men and women are better and holier than the men and women of the Christians? If they have not a *better* class of people, in what respect does their uninspired creed protect them against dangerous elements, that our inspired Scriptures do not? But surely, "*The creed will bind the people more closely together, than the Scriptures alone.*" Ah! this is the most extravagant and untenable claim of all!

The Bible alone will show its sufficiency by binding the people together and to Christ, as no creed can. If a man be a Christian, is he not a branch of the Vine? and can there be a relationship closer to Christ than that of the branch to the Vine? Moreover, is not the relationship to another branch of the same Vine just as close as that of either branch to the Vine itself? By this argument, then, is not the one branch of the True Vine just as closely related to another branch of the same Vine as to that vine itself? Can the creed more closely or intensely cement or bind the Christian to Christ or his fellow-Christian, than he is already bound by the Scriptures and the Holy Ghost? Does not every denomination consent that the regenerated young convert is in Christ, and that his love, as a youthful disciple of Jesus, is perfectly intense for all his Master's dear children? But what does he know of the creed, or what thought has he bestowed upon it? It has had no agency in his regeneration, or in binding his heart, with such disinterested devotion, to the followers of Jesus. Can the creed-monger, with a shadow of truth in his heart, look into the face of the young convert and say in the language of the above claim, "*The creed will bind your heart more closely to the family of Christ than it is already bound by the Bible and the Spirit?* There would not be a particle of truth in such an assertion, nor is there more in the exact language of the claim, as stated above.

But let us press the argument further, in the light of historical fact. Methodism started on its (in many respects blessed career) as *one*, but who can easily number the divisions of Methodism to-day? Has the creed held the Methodist family together? Had they taken the Bible alone, Methodism would be *one* to-day! Is united Methodism better than divided Methodism? The efforts for the unification of Methodism indicate that they think so. Then are the Scriptures alone better for Methodism than the creed. That which the Bible could have prevented the Bible can best undo. We commend it to our good Methodist friends in their commendable effort at unification.

Presbyterianism started as *one*, but to-day the general body has 50 heads, each one of which is crowned with a creed. The creed has failed, manifestly, in binding together the family of Presbyterianism?

Has the binding and cementing power of the creed been any better with the other denominations? Why commend to us the creed *as a binding force in Christian fellowship for all God's family*, when it utterly fails to bind together in oneness a small fraction of that family? With our eyes on miserable failures of the creed in this direction, it hardly seems less than ridiculous audacity to press upon us the same pitiful agency as a means to a stronger and more fervent union! If the Bible alone is insufficient as an agency of union, for what is the creed more fully sufficient and remarkable than as a wedge to divide and mangle the Church of Christ! How different the experience of the Christians! With the Scriptures alone as their rule of faith and practice, they began life 75 years ago. They have never suffered a division in their history and are as heartily united in their work, faith and fellowship as any people, or any branch of any people, on earth to-day. The Bible has not divided us, nor is it likely to do so, but it has bound us in one blessed fellowship, as it would the universal Church, if the creed was thrown to the winds or given to the flames. The Church is in a shattered, bleeding condition to-day, expending more of its moral force and substantial means in fostering and nourishing its divisions than in performing its legitimate work of converting the world. If Christ organized but one Church and did not provide for a second, then the fullest union and co-operation of that one Church is desirable and obligatory! On no one creed can it unite its scattered forces. On the Bible alone and under the banner of the Cross, with Jesus as the only leader, there could be no difficulty in the way.

"CHRISTIAN CHARACTER THE TEST."

By Rev. J. W. Osborn, Ph. D., Swansea, Mass.

That "Christian character is the only test of fellowship" is uniformly regarded as one of the fundamental principles of the communion of churches known as Christians.

In the book entitled the "Principles and Government of the Christian Church," published by the authority of the "General Convention" "composed of representatives from all the Christian Conferences in the Southern States," is a direction that "in the organization of a church," among the articles of agreement to be signed, shall be one stating that "Christian character, or vital piety, is the true Scriptural test of fellowship and of church membership." In the chapter on the "Principles of the Church," in the same volume, is a statement in these words, varying slightly from those just quoted: "Christian character, or vital piety, is a just, and should be the only, test of fellowship, or of church membership."

However plain a proposition may be, an occasional re-statement is necessary, both to draw attention anew to the truth enunciated, and to adjust its expression to varying modes of thought. Different communities view a subject in different aspects, and it must be so presented as to be adapted to the apprehension of all. And in successive generations the evolution of thought must at every stage be met by a fresh presentation of the principle to be taught.

"Spiritual things are spiritually discerned." The ability to understand a statement includes the capacity to conceive the fact or principle concerning which the statement is made.

Of education and culture, a gentleman blind from his birth, remarked that "the word 'red' seemed to him to signify something like a cane; "and the word 'green' something like the music of an organ." Some men attach a vague meaning, or a significance radically false, to language, which for the comprehension of other men, is sufficiently explicit. If there is no moral infirmity or spiritual obtuseness to prevent a clear perception, there may be misapprehension resulting from the necessary ambiguity of language. Perhaps for this reason, an alternative expression is used in the thesis—"Christian character, or vital piety."

The word "Christian" and the phrase "Christian character" are used with great latitude of meaning.

Sometimes men are styled "Christians" because they live in a land where christianity, instead of Mahomedanism or Paganism, is generally regarded as the true system of religion. And there are many advantages in living in a community where Christian conceptions of what is manly and becoming pervade society to a degree sufficient not only to secure the enactment of laws designed to restrain if not reform the criminal, to protect the weak from the strong and unscrupulous, and to unite order with liberty; but so to promote honesty, benevolence and purity, that one seldom needs the protection of law. In such a state of society the worst man, though he may utterly repudiate the claims of christianity, and treat its truths with bitter scorn, enjoys a multitude of advantages due to its beneficent influence: if in prison he is far more fortunate than though a prisoner in any other land. Though he may forget God, the Gospel affords him, unconsciously, blessings without number and beyond price. But his advantages may fail to make him morally better; they may possibly make him worse. The fact that one's birthright involves great privileges may not prevent him from selling it, even for a "mess of pottage." *Opportunity* is not "Christian character." Among all forms of religious belief, it is probably true that Protestant Christianity, as deducted from the New Testament, alone recognizes a distinction, broad, deep and radical, between a merely nominal or national religion, and personal piety. In the absence of contrary evidence, it is assumed that every Moslem is a "true believer," every Roman Catholic a "faithful son of the church." But the New Testament treats religion as *character;* and character is *individual.*

In some instances men are regarded as Christians merely because they are not guilty of gross violations of morality, according to the particular ideal of the community concerned: an ideal varying as the temperature of the zones, and fickle as the winds.

The conception of character underlying the assumption is negative; but in morals, as elsewhere, "nature abhors a vacuum." Character is positive.

To suppose that one becomes a Christian merely by participating in religious ceremonies, is to confound rites with righteousness: as did those who plotted the death of our Saviour, but would not enter Pilate's judgment hall, lest they should be defiled, and unfit to eat the passover. The character developed in habitual performances regarded as sacred may be either that of a hypocrite who deceives others, or of a formalist who deceives himself.

Christian character is sometimes regarded as an accumulation of creditable deeds. Good actions must never be decried; the world needs more, not less, of them. No infidel ever harmed the church of Christ as it has been injured by those who "profess that they know God, but in works deny Him, being abominable, and disobedient, and unto every good work reprobate." But generous actions may spring from ungenerous motives; the kiss of pretended affection may be given by a Judas. Not long ago, the

Superintendent of a Sunday School, who was also habitually a participant in prayer meetings, was convicted of fraud, and committed to prison. After his mask was so suddenly removed, he declared that he never believed in the religion he professed. He had pretended to be converted and to be very zealous, because in the church with which he united there was a wealthy gentleman who took much interest in worthy young men, and established several in business; and this imposter hoped to secure similar help. Felix often communed with Paul, hoping the prisoner would offer a bribe for his freedom.

Good deeds may be the indices of Christian graces, a strong and lofty pyramid, built up of "living stones" and resting on the "Rock of Ages." To the faith which constitutes the Christian, may be added "virtue, knowledge, temperance, patience, godliness, brotherly-kindness, charity." Or a character may resemble a cairn, which, in some countries marks the spot where a murder has been committed and the victim buried; a heap of stones carelessly tossed together without order; worthless pebbles over a decaying corpse—the memorial of a crime.

That which is built up from without is artificial and mechanical; a genuine religious character is an organism. The dead branch may serve as a rod; only the living branch grows; the Power that caused Aaron's rod to bud alone can impart life to the dead.

Facts pertaining to Christianity may be perceived with no more moral responsiveness than is involved in the perception that the tides flow and the grass grows. Grand truths essential to the Gospel as the revelation of God to man, and the recognition of God by man,—that God is love, and that He sent His Son to save men from the power and guilt of sin,—may convince the understanding, and yet no more awaken the slumbering soul than does the assurance that "a whole is equal to all its parts." The "golden rule" may be accepted by the reason as the true principle of conduct, and yet have no more effect upon the hardened, selfish heart than does the "rule of three." The seat of character is deeper than the intellect. And yet religion is not mere feeling. Love is not *emotion* but *devotion*.

The winters of some portions of our Northern States are occasionally interrupted by "thaws." The snow dissolves, the ice melts, the frost "leaves the ground;" a stranger would suppose that spring had come. But a single night brings back all the rigor of winter. The "cold waves" of air from polar regions bind up the streams, and harden the earth like a rock. So there are men (affected perhaps by the example of others), whose hearts seem ready to yield to the beams of the Sun of Righteousness: their icy natures appear to melt;— but soon the wintry blasts rage with all their former violence. When the soul in reality yields to the power of the Sun, "the winter is past, the rain is over and gone, the flowers appear on the earth, the time of the singing of birds is come."

By "Christian character," when specified as the "test of fellowship," is not meant mature spiritual development. The apostle who urges growth "in grace and the knowledge of our Lord and Saviour Jesus Christ" is speaking "to them that *have* obtained like precious faith with us." As the mother nourishes and protects the infant, so the church receives those who are "babes in Christ;" and within its pale they "grow up in Him."

To attempt to fix the conditions of fellowship in such way as to require a certain degree of improvement in propriety of manners, or of spiritual growth, would be impracticable. It would be impossible to determine the size of the cairn in one case, or the height of the pyramid in the other. The qualifications for admission must be recognized more distinctly and definitely.

By "Christian character" is meant THAT CHARACTER WHICH IS IMMEDIATELY ATTAINED IN THE EXERCISE OF SAVING FAITH IN THE LORD JESUS CHRIST.

The exercise of faith involves the surrender of ourselves to Him, including not only repentance, but obedience and trust; if we yield ourselves to the Lord, we heed alike His precepts and His promises.

Impenitence is the refusal to surrender our will (that is ourselves) to Christ. Hence He said to some who rejected Him, "Ye WILL NOT come to Me, that ye might have life;" and He gave assurance of the highest knowledge to "any man that WILLETH to do God's will." In the choice of the "good part" the human will is both actively and passively devoted to the Divine will. In the Lord's Prayer we are taught to say " *Thy will be done* in earth as it is in heaven." We pray that God's will may be done BY ourselves and all men. In the garden of Gethsemane our Saviour used the same language,—" *Thy will be done;* but here it is modified by the words preceding—" If this cup may not pass from me except I drink it." As His disciples, we, even though "the flesh is weak," desire that God's will be done IN us; or as expressed in the familiar verse—

" Thy will be done, though in mine own undoing."

The choice of God's will as the rule of life is MAN'S ACT. But more than this is involved in "passing from death unto life." When Solomon dedicated the temple to the Most High, He accepted it, and it was filled with His glory. As a "temple" the Christian is dedicated to the Lord's service, and the Holy Spirit accepts and fills that temple. As light supersedes darkness, so the Divine Presence in the devoted heart dwells where before earthly and sinful loves had supreme sway. The affections are renewed by the grace and power of the Saviour.

So that "Christian character or vital piety" is not merely man's voluntary submission to the will of God; it is the product of the unresisted operation of the Divine Spirit on the heart. "As many as received Him, to them gave He power [the prerogative] to become the sons of God." They are "born of God." "Vital piety" is not the result of the gift of a new nature, but of being "partakers of the Divine nature." There is no *delay* in the entrance of the Holy Spirit. Simultaneously with the removal of the obstruction, the sunlight which bathed the outer wall, illuminates the room. The penitent surrender of the will to God secures forgiveness; and forgiveness must of necessity be instantaneous.

But, although the Lord knows *when* the door of the soul is open to receive Him, and instantly enters, it may be long before men are convinced that the "wicked man has turned away from his wickedness." Even the disciples suspected the genuineness of the conversion of Saul of Tarsus, until Barnabas, that "Son of Consolation," interposed to satisfy them that their former persecutor was "a new man in Christ Jesus." As soon as the Christian church has reason to believe, "in the judgment of charity," that one is "born of God," it bids him welcome as a member of the "household of faith."

The declaration that Christian character "is the test of fellowship and of church membership," implies that all who are regarded as worthy of "fellowship" as followers of Christ, are also fit to be members of the church. While a *formal* distinction between such "fellowship" and "church membership" is recognized, no *moral* difference is acknowledged. If one is a Christian, he is not only to be loved and trusted as such outside the door of the church, but within it.

The objection is sometimes urged that the churches of the Christian connection have no way of determining whether an applicant for membership *possesses* a Christian character. And it must be conceded that it is not as easy to decide that a man has a "clean heart" as it is that he has clean hands; or that he loves God as that he has confessed to a priest. It may readily be proved that a candidate for admission to the Lord's table has been immersed in water, when "the washing of regeneration and the renewing of the Holy Ghost" may not be obvious. If merely ritualistic conditions are regarded, it is easy to determine who may, and who may not, be admitted to the privileges of members of the church. But as regards the special objection urged, on the point where the difficulty lies, the churches of the Christian connection do not differ, *in any respect whatever*, from such other evangelical churches as rigorously apply doctrinal tests. In one case, Christian character alone is the criterion; in the other Christian character *and belief in certain doctrines*. If *one* has the duty of deciding whether a candidate possesses the requisite spiritual qualification, the *other* has that duty, and the additional task of determining whether the applicant—(in many cases a person of immature years, or of habits of mind totally unfitted to discuss abstract themes)—has correct opinions on points of doctrine concerning which the best, the most learned and the wisest of men widely differ; perhaps on subjects including the "things which the angels desire to look into." No church has exclusive possession of spiritual mercury, to separate the precious gold from the worthless dross.

As an incidental aid in determining one's spiritual fitness for admittance to the church, the applicant might, without violation of the principle propounded, be questioned on those truths universally recognized as essential to the Christian religion. And doctrinal *tests* are regarded as objectionable when applied to opinions concerning which men of acknowledged piety *differ*, and not to truths in which they *agree*. VITAL ORTHODOXY is involved in "vital piety."

To guard against the danger of a misguided and false application of the principle of tolerance now under discussion, it may be necessary to remark that the arrogant and offensive dogmatist, who vehemently urges his pet theories to the annoyance of the brethren, as distinct from the faithful and affectionate presentation of religious truth in its various aspects and applications, cannot claim admittance to the church on the ground of "Christian character." He habitually violates the "golden rule," and the precept to "follow after the things which make for peace, and the things whereby one may edify another."

Respecting the "ordinances" of the church, it may suffice to remark that Christian character is the title alike to baptism and the Lord's Supper. These ordinances are evidently designed as helps to the Christian in living a devoted life. The memory of the Lord Jesus is precious to all who serve Him; and the communion service makes vivid the conception of His love and sacrifice. The value of the observance does not depend on any antecedent ordinance. Who could imagine our Saviour reproving a "weak" disciple for REMEMBERING HIM, or for seeking by the help of the memorial supper to realize more clearly His words of grace and His power to save from sin? The question concerning the relative order in which the two ordinances should be observed, is of no more significance than the child's query—"Shall I kiss mamma *before* or after I say 'Good morning'?" The ordinances are of value simply as they serve to express and increase the heart's devotion to the Lord; and any merely mechanical, formal or arbitrary adjustment of them must tend to rob them of their power to bless the soul.

"The cardinal principles of the Christian church" are intimately related. Logically, they stand or fall together. As a sect that rejects Him who is "the only Head of the Church" cannot with propriety assume His name, so those who decline "party names" should welcome to their particular spiritual household all who "are of the household of God."

The Convention, by an ample statement of the "Sentiments of the Church," at once indicates the doctrine that is usually preached by Christian ministers, and to some extent guards its purity. With an evangelical ministry and a regenerate membership, no fear is felt of "false doctrine, heresy and schism."

The substance of this paper, written in compliance with a request to define "What we, as a Church, mean by the declaration that 'Christian character, or vital piety, is a just, and should be the only test,'" may be thus briefly stated: Christian character as instantaneously attained in the exercise of true faith in the Lord Jesus Christ, by a spiritual birth effected by the power of the Holy Ghost, is the essential prerequisite for admission to the ordinances and fellowship of the Church.

PRIVATE JUDGMENT, THE RIGHT AND DUTY OF EVERY BELIEVER.

Sermon by Prof. MARTYN SUMMERBELL, M. A., of New York City.

Then Peter and the other apostles answered and said: "We ought to obey God rather than men." (Acts v : 29.)

When the Christian Church in America advances, as one of its cardinal principles, the doctrine of the right of private judgment in matters of opinion, it is simply repeating one of the fundamental principles of the Protestant Reformation, and also reaffirming the declaration of the Apostles, when summoned before the Sanhedrin for preaching Jesus—" We ought to obey God rather than men." Somewhere, humanly speaking, a final appeal in matters of religious debate must lie.

In the judgment of the Apostles, and in ours, that high tribunal is, not the Sanhedrin, supreme authority for the Jewish hierarchy though it be; not a bench of bishops clad with Apostolic powers as legitimate successors and representatives of the Apostles; not an infallible Pope, lording it over God's heritage with *ex cathedra* ecclesiastical fulminations; not any man, nor any body of men, acting in their own authority or by authority of others, but simply and only the conscience of the individual believer, as it hearkens for the voice of God, and reverently endeavors to obey his word. Believing that right there, in the individual conscience, resides the court of last resort, the Christian Church, in common with all Protestants, asserts private judgment to be the right and duty of every believer. In explanation of this principle we will consider the view of the Christian Church respecting private judgment and the methods of its exercise, so far as these affect the churches and individual Christians.

"We must obey God rather than men," say Peter and the other apostles. Please observe the nature of this protest and the grounds on which it rests. Peter and the others have come to open conflict with the highest authority known in the Jewish nation. The great Sanhedrin, which has full charge of all religious affairs, which settles all disputes, which punishes with stoning, with beheading, with hanging or with burning, has commanded them not to speak or teach in the name of Jesus.

It now accuses them of contempt for its august decree, and complains that they have filled Jerusalem with their doctrine, with evident intention of making the Holy City, and the Sanhedrin itself, guilty of the blood of Jesus. The charge is explicit and grave. If substantiated, it implies on the part of the Apostles a disregard for the religious convictions of their countrymen, as well as scorn for the Sanhedrin itself, which sways civil and ecclesiastical powers, and resistance to which, in Jewish eyes, combines sacrilege with high treason. What shall they answer? We listen and catch the substance of their plea—"We must obey God rather than men."

Here by implication we find a claim that God speaks to men, and to individual men. In some way the Divine Will penetrates the secret places of their hearts. They have felt God's power, heard His speech, and realized the momentum of

—— " Truths that wake
To perish never."

So fixed is their assurance that it was God

talking with them, that they are constrained to relax their customary submission to authorities, and to expose themselves to every trial and every terror of persecution, rather than ignore the evident will of the Almighty. They must uphold the truth as God has revealed it to them. So they affirm and reaffirm—"We must obey God rather than men."

Now God speaks to men in various ways. Some truth he makes known through the intuitions. Advanced philosophers now claim that there are moral intuitions, as well as those of time and space. We know that effect follows cause, and so also we know that a grateful response to a kindness is right, and that neglect and ingratitude are wrong. We know that the whole is greater than any of its parts, and equally well we know, and in the same way, that moral responsibility involves freedom. Sin to be sin, sin which weighs us down, is not the sin which we are compelled to commit, but the sin which we choose to commit. The good man of the house, who defends his domicile from a burglar, is not guilty when he shoots the intruder. Because he acts under compulsion, the voice within his soul commends him, and the innate sense of justice, as crystallized in common law, sustains him.

And God speaks to men through sense perception. A universe stretches before the thinking soul, vast, complicate, and yet in every part ruled by exact principle, which some call law, but which those who walk with God perceive to be the will and direction of the Creator. Out of this universe of spaces and forces and worlds and living creatures, and man made in the image of God, stream influences which, as the soul wills, may move it toward good or toward evil. From this outer world come appeals to passion, lures toward self-centred greed, and incentives to vaulting ambition. From the same outer world come also combinations of form and color and useful purpose, which rouse the soul to appreciation of delight in beauty; associations which become incentives to tender and unselfish affection; views of order and adaptation and correlation of plan and accomplishment throughout the creation of matter and mind, which insensibly lead up from admiration for the works of nature to a devout reliance on nature's God. The charm of the summer landscape, the voice of the birds in forest and meadow chanting their morning psalm, the cool hush of evening, when the starry heavens invite to peaceful meditation on man's weakness as a child of the dust, and his infinite majesty as a child of God, the moral questions which agitate our social world, summoning us to decide for justice against oppression, for righteousness against iniquity, for truth against lies; all these are Divine voices, summoning the soul to cast off its shackles and stand in all its possible glory as heir of eternity.

But chief of all, God speaks to man in His Son and in His Holy Word. The Apostles, as disciples, sit at Jesus' feet. Wonderful the effect of His presence on all who approach Him. Rude officers of the temple, sent to apprehend Him, return saying,— "Never man spake like this man." Under His teaching the toilers of the sea become fishers of men—Christ's love in their hearts, God's word on their lips. They follow not cunningly devised fables, but are eye-witnesses of His majesty. All the divinity in their souls, pledge of their kinship with

God, responds to Christ's gentleness and purity and truth.

By the wisdom which illuminated the darkest problems, and by the power which ruled the bodies and souls of men, they recognized Him as the Messiah long sought, the Son of the living God. After His resurrection and ascension, if ever a doubt had beclouded judgment, the outpouring of the Holy Ghost on the day of Pentecost swept it away. What He had declared to them was the teaching of God. They could not gainsay it. They could not bury it out of remembrance. Though all all courts should enjoin them, and all thrones command them to silence, they are constrained to say—" We must obey God rather than men."

In the centuries, however, since Christ has ascended to glory, God speaks to man most clearly by His Holy Spirit through the Scriptures. These embody so much of His purpose as He has determined to disclose. They reveal the course of His gracious providence in the history of nations and men. They establish the basis of moral and civil law. They declare His purpose of amazing grace in the gift of His Son, by whose life, and death, and resurrection, sinners have promise of redemption and everlasting life. Surely this Bible is a light that shineth in a dark place, until the day dawn and the day-star arise in your hearts. Speak of diversity; sixty-six books go to its making, involving all styles from the simple speech of shepherds to the profoundest thoughts that surge in the mind of a Job, an Isaiah, a Paul or a John in the rapture of his apocalyptic vision; and yet from the initial *Beth*, in the first book, to the *Nu* final in the last, there breathes one moral purpose, one Divine aim in helping humanity, one thought of God as man's best friend and father. Test this statement as closely as you will. Make it a study to learn what thought of morality and Deity prevails where this book is read and believed, and what, where it is driven out of common life and common mind. Where it is not read you shall find morality at a low ebb, honor a term of empty fuss and swagger, virtue a pretence, and God and heaven names to swear by in every breath. But where this book is read and loved, lying and trickery are hated, men can trust their fel-

Private Judgment. 109

lows in deed or in word, and life and religion become sacred under the conviction of God's searching knowledge of iniquity, and His certain recompense for goodness.

And all these voices of God speak to the individual man. The world within and the world without to me are darkness until God brings me light. The Apostles in the lesson were responsible for the truths which God had set in celestial radiance before the eyes of their soul. Remark this in this conviction of the revelation of Christ. Peter was convinced of Christ's Messiahship. As God had traced with his finger the Ten Words on Moses' stone tables, so he had written this knowledge of Christ on Peter's heart. "Blessed art thou, Simon Bar-Jona," said Jesus, "for flesh and blood hath not revealed it unto thee, but my Father, which is in heaven." Others had seen the Lord, had witnessed his miracles and heard His gracious words, but all these things God had set in order in Peter's soul, so that he beheld the Saviour's glory. It is much the same with all the varieties of truth through which God speaks to us. Here is this Bible. How rare the book. And it is most rare in this, that as we read it God brings us continually to richer treasures of knowledge. The famous Dr. Kennicott was thirty years writing his commentary. It was his practice to ride out with his wife on pleasant days, when she would read the portion of Scripture on which he was preparing the comment. At last the book was done, the last page written. As usual they take their daily ride.

"What book shall I take to-day, Doctor?" asks his faithful wife.

"Oh!" said he, "Let us begin the Bible." After thirty years of closest scrutiny it was still full of interest, possibly replete with profounder interest than ever before.

So Luther studied the Bible diligently and assiduously. He pursued a special investigation of Romans and Galatians. With his mind intent on the Sacred Word he goes to Rome. As yet old associations and teachings cramp his intellect and fetter his judgment. Yonder is Pilate's staircase. The story goes that it has been translated by miracle from Jerusalem to Rome, and that those marble steps were trodden by our blessed Lord, when he was led into Pilate's judgment hall. Pilgrims in Rome from every part of the world believe the fable, and so crawl up the staircase on their knees. Luther believes and acts with the rest, only he climbs but half way. See him there, painfully mounting, like a slave bowed under a burden. Superstition crushes him down. But see! he rises. He stands upon his feet. He turns and hurries like a man down the stair. How now, brother Martin? God has spoken to him. As it had been the voice of an angel this text flashed upon his mind, "The just shall live by faith;" and God then and there taught him its application, that he was not to trust for salvation in dead works, or in penance, or in mortifications of the flesh, but only in faith in the Son of God. That was God's revelation to Luther's soul, God's enforcement of Biblical truth to set him free from the bondage of error.

In reference to all these teachings of God, in reference to general truth, and especially in reference to truth as it is revealed in Holy Scripture, it is the doctrine of the Protestant Reformation, and a doctrine particularly emphasized by the Christian Church, that the interpretation of truth by private judgment is the right and duty of every believer.

On this very point hinges the question between Protestanism and Romanism. The practice of Rome through all the years since the growth of the Papacy has been to rely upon the Scriptures and tradition. The Bible was the *regula fidei*, the rule of faith: but so only as it was interpreted by the fathers and the church. The true faith, according to Rome, is not the faith which the believer reads for himself in the Word of God, but what the great councils in creeds and decrees declare the Bible to teach; or what the Pope, sitting in Peter's chair as vicegerent of Christ, pronounces to be the faith of the church.

So reads the creed of Pope Pius IV: "I also admit the Holy Scriptures according to that sense which our holy mother, the Church, has held, and does hold, to which it belongs to judge of the true sense and interpretation of the Scriptures. Neither will I ever take and interpret them otherwise than according to the unanimous consent of the fathers."

With similar reliance on tradition the Council of Trent denounces every one who, "confiding in his own judgment, shall dare to wrest the sacred Scriptures to his own sense of them," and proceeds to declare it is the right of holy mother church—"to judge of the true meaning and interpretation of Sacred Writ."

Luther, Calvin, Zwingle, and all the Reformers met this position with the challenge of absolute contradiction. They charged that to entrust the church with the right to decide for the believer what the Bible teaches would stultify conscience, and subordinate the Bible to the church. Instead of this the Bible should be supreme, controversies should be decided, not by Bible and tradition, but by Bible only, and believers should seek its meaning not from the parish priest, but from diligent study of the book itself as interpreted by the Holy Spirit. This is the theory of Protestanism, which all the great symbols state in enequivocal terms. The Augsburg Confession, 1530, beside quoting various Scriptures to substantiate the right of churches to refuse submission to bishops, who teach or determine anything contrary to the gospel, quotes from Augustine: "Neither must we subscribe to Catholic bishops, if they chance to err, or determine anything contrary to the canonical divine scriptures."

The Formula of Concord, 1576, begins with this unmistakable language: "We believe, confess and teach that the only true rule and norm, according to which all dogmas and all doctors ought to be determined and judged, is no other whatever than the prophetic and apostolic writings of the Old and of the New Testament."

The First Helvetic Confession, 1536, states the doctrine briefly but clearly—I translate from the parallel Latin and German document, Art. 2: "These holy and sacred Scriptures shall be interpreted and explained by themselves only, under the guidance of faith and love."

The Westminster Confession, which devotes its first chapter to an exhaustive discussion of Holy Scripture, in the 10th Article, uses this explicit language: "The Supreme Judge by which all controversies of religion are to be determined, and all decrees of councils, opinions of ancient writers, doctrines of men and private spirits, are to be examined, and in whose sentence we are to rest, can be no other but the Holy Spirit speaking in Scripture."

Thus church after church, breaking away from the thraldom of the papacy, asserted its independence. In every case the appeal lay to Scripture and conscience. As Schleiermacher draws the distinction: "Protestanism makes the relation of the individual to the church dependent on his relation to Christ; Catholicism, *vice versa*, makes the relation of the individual to Christ dependent on his relation to the church."

Of this latter arrangement the Reformers would have none. Their final plea was an explicit declaration of the Word of God, no matter what the Church had said. With refreshing uniformity they denied the right of any person or persons, singly or collectively, individually or officially, to interpret that book for any believer so as to bind his conscience. Contrariwise they affirmed that God had invested every Christian with the right to search the Scriptures for himself, and moreover, lays it upon him as a sacred trust to investigate and establish the grounds of his individual faith.

Protestants claim that private judgment

is a right because of the glorious freedom of the Christian faith. Through all the gospels and the epistles rings the triumphant song of liberty in Christ. Old things are passed away; the cumbrous law, the commandment of death, the subjection to place in the temple worship, and to time in the set festivals, and to form in an ironclad ritual, and to a man in the priest standing at the altar, demanding that all who approach God shall send their petitions through him; and behold, all things are become new; a new temple, the retreat of a true heart in which God dwells by his Spirit, a new church in which every believer is himself a king and a priest unto God, a new law under which sacrifices are not the blood of bulls and goats, but the spiritual sacrifices of love and faith and penitence and brotherly kindness, and a new relationship in which man no longer stands apart from God, but draws nigh by a blessed faith, trusting in but one Mediator and Intercessor, Jesus the eternal Son of God. This glorious freedom releases from all spiritual subjugation. When men attempt to govern the church by an infallible law, or by an infallible pope, the Christian declares the attempt usurpation,. and resists it. If they meet in councils and interpret his faith for him he hesitates, he compares their teaching with the Bible, and if to his mind it is error, he rejects it. He has this privilege. He is a free man in Christ.

Private judgment is a right moreover from the necessities of the case. Religion is of all things individual and personal. Patriotism, family affection, public spirit, all these affect other men. So religion affects other men, but not primarily. It begins with God, and its relation to other men is secondary to this, which is always chief. Into this relationship with God all outside influences that enter with pretended authority are intrusion and meddlesomeness. "Every one of us," exclaims St. Paul, "shall give account of himself to God." With noble scorn he asks of those who question and disturb the brethren: "Who art thou that judgest another man's servant? to his own master he standeth or falleth." Because man must answer for himself he must decide for himself. He cannot plead at the judgment that he went astray because he was led astray by the church, or by the minister or by the creed. The responsibility of his soul's salvation rests with himself, and it is his right to know for himself from the Word of God if, or if not, he is following the upward path.

Private judgment is a right which is confirmed by Holy Scripture. Nowhere is it written that God's word is addressed to the exclusive control of the priesthood, or of the church, to be doled out to the people as the authorities may decide expedient. In place of that it is given to the people, and they are strictly commanded to search and know the truth. God through Isaiah declares—"If they speak not according to this word it is because there is no light in them." Jesus commends the Rabbis who search the scriptures, and St. Luke praises the Bereans, as "more noble" than those of Thessalonica "in that they received the word with all readiness of mind, and searched the Scriptures daily whether these things were so." So again, the epistles are directly dedicated to the brethren. Look up their inscriptions and you find them written, not to councils and conferences and minister's associations, but "to the saints," "to the called of Jesus Christ," "to the beloved of God" and "to the faithful in Christ Jesus."

And this right of private judgment of Holy Scripture, which frees the people from the dictation of ecclesiastics, is further established since the Bible, far from permitting teachers and preachers to consent together to decide what the people shall believe, authorizes the people to judge for themselves the teaching of their teachers, whether it be according to the word of God.

When the Rabbis refused to acknowledge his Messiahship, Jesus turned to the peasants of Galilee to decide between him and the lawyers, warning them meanwhile against the leaven of the Scribes and Pharisees, and against false prophets, who were to be discerned by their fruits. So St. Paul wrote to the Thessalonians of prophesyings;—" Prove all things, hold fast that which is good." Here is intimated the double process of private judgment; first, a rule of comparison by which good is to be determined, *i. e.*, the Holy Word; and, second, an untrammelled conscience, capable of making judgment and of rejecting error. Another instance, if anything still more positive, appears in the admonition to the Galatian brethren, who were directed to investigate the claims of Apostles:—"Though we or an angel from heaven," says St. Paul, "preach any other gospel unto you than that which we have preached unto you, let him be accursed." The Galatians are to test their teachers by the gospel. If the teachers teach the word, well. If they deny the word as it is recognized by the consciences of the brethren, then they are to have no countenance. A direction to the same purport occurs in the epistle, where St. John advises: "Beloved, believe not every spirit, but try the spirits whether they are of God: because many false prophets are gone out into the world." Private judgment consequently is a right, a right which every believer should maintain, and which he should permit no man, nor any body of men to abrogate or infringe.

But private judgment is more than a right, it is the duty of every believer. This is true first of all, because the Bible, being addressed to all, should be heeded by all. We may look upon Holy Scripture as God's message to his people. Now when I receive a letter from a friend I read it for myself and form my own opinion of my friend's feelings and desires. If it is written in a foreign language, I may engage some person to translate it for me, but I would not be obliged to him, if, in place of translating my whole letter, he should give me a scrap here and a scrap there, telling me that these contained all that was of importance. My respect for my friend, my respect for myself would demand the whole letter. Is it not the same with God's message to His children? It is given us as a whole, and even if we cannot read it in the original tongues, we can read it in good translations, and we owe it to our Heavenly Father, who has honored us by committing it to our charge, to read it and to understand it as a whole, bestowing on its perusal our best judgment, and suffering no man to interpose anything whatever in its place.

And private judgment is a duty also, since by its exercise only can we arrive at a rich and intelligent comprehension of the Word of God. With Biblical study, as with other pursuits, we are interested most, and we learn most in that to which we have devoted time and diligent labor. Second-hand knowledge of Scripture, like all second-hand knowledge, is pretentious ignorance. How shall you prepare your son for a counting house? Will it suffice to provide him lecturers who shall tell him about penmanship and book-keeping and figures? Even admitting that the lecturers proposed were the very best, and would teach approved principles only, you would require something far more practical. The mind cannot be filled by a force pump. Boys learn by digging out principles, practicing penmanship, keeping books by single and double entry, and working out the problems in fractions and interest and proportion and mensuration. And by the same practical law he will grow wise in Sripture who compares Scripture with Scripture, analyzing, arranging, re-arranging and judging doctrines and opinions according to his best understanding of what God would teach. Who does anything less than this, when he can study the Bible, is guilty of starving his own soul.

And still again, private judgment is the duty of every believer, since, as we have before seen God, speaks through his Word, and the message, reaching the believer, is God's very own, the signification of which he must himself finally determine; with, I grant, the aid of all resources at command, and yet with his own conscience, in the light of the Holy Spirit, as final arbiter.

Lord Macaulay, in one of his essays, wisely remarks: "There are two intelligible and consistent courses which may be followed with respect to the exercise of private judgment, the course of the Romanist who interdicts private judgment because of its inevitable inconveniences, and the course of the Protestant, who permits private judgment in spite of its inevitable inconveniences."

Lord Macaulay admits no middle course. There is no middle course. It must be either conscience answerable to God or else conscience answerable, mediately or immediately, to the priest. No need to annul the law to betray it. Tyrants can tyrannize under the most republican of republican forms of government by interpreting the laws at their option. And the Bible can be made inoperative, while it is seemingly honored, by men, who, usurping authority in its interpretation, actually assume the authority which belong to Scripture itself.

The Apostles in the lesson felt this thoroughly. Why not refer their heaven-sent message to the scrutiny of the Great Sanhedrin? These greybeards were wise, were learned, were after some sort conscientious; but to have trusted their judgment finally would have been to obey men rather than God.

It is the same when I bring my Bible to any ecclesiastical body and abide by its declaration of the meaning. If I rest upon the decision of conference, convention, synod or council, and abide by it when my conscience, from the light shed from the page of the Bible, teaches me otherwise, I betray my stewardship, I obey men rather than God. This I cannot do. This you cannot do. We must read the Scriptures for ourselves, in the light of the best helps which the age can furnish, with the counsel of the wisest teachers to be obtained; but after all has been said, duty compels the final decision of faith to rest with the individual conscience.

In this there can be no option. "We must obey God rather than man."

The Christian Church, which teaches the right and duty of private judgment, recognizes that so large a right involves care and discretion in its exercise. As a rule without exceptions, privilege multiplies obligations. If Christ mercifully endows his disciples with the blessed boon of Gospel liberty, it is not that every man shall be a law unto himself, the Bible is the standard of faith and practice; not that men shall degrade liberty to license, the tenderness of Christian love is still to restrain disorders; not that the peace of the church shall be endangered, but instead, that all, taking the same law, and drawing nearer to God, may recognize their common brotherhood in Jesus.

Exercising their right of private judgment, therefore, believers will consider the unity of Scripture. God gives them the Bible as a whole.

In and through all there must be harmony, not confusion; agreement, not contradiction. A true interpretation of God's Word, therefore, will not be hasty, but one which compares book with book, passage with passage, and so reaches what I may term the heart of Scripture rather than its husk, and the spirit rather than the letter.

The believer exercising private judgment will also hold fast to the proportion of Scripture. Some truths God has revealed plainly. They stand out on the general background of revelation like the brightest stars in the azure sky. It is safe for the Christian to believe that God has emphasized what He desired to emphasize, and that it has pleased Him to leave in comparative obscurity what He reveals partially. And it is safe also to follow this scale of scriptural proportion in teaching and preaching. We can insist on the general acceptance of what God has made very plain in His Word; and if, beyond that, He has made something quite plain to us, let it be plain to us; but the attempt by any person to coerce the conscience of others, where the Bible is silent, or where its expressions leave room for honest difference of opinion, is to be resisted by good Protestants and Christians as Peter resisted the Sanhedrin, and as Luther resisted the pope.

Private judgment, however, should not be

exclusive. To be judgment it must traverse the whole field that is in debate. In the broad sweep of questions and probabilities it will place much stress on the general faith of Christians. It may at once be conceded that individually they hold countless errors, but if God speaks to them, and if they drink faith from the pure fountain of Scripture revelation, the chances greatly favor that when they are agreed they are agreed upon the truth. A message that conflicts with the universal faith of christendom must not complain if it is treated like a suspected character. It may be held with great certainty of conviction, but that it is unique, discordant, erratic, seems to indicate that it is from the devil. When that man at Pocasset believed that God had directed him to sacrifice his child, the common sense of his Christian neighbors and of the village pastor would have taught him that such an impulse was from beneath, and not from above.

And furthermore, private judgment, claiming so much for itself, will grant to others all that it asks. Private judgment knocks at the door of the local church. It holds opinions which it has a right to hold, gained from independent investigation of the Bible. The church, truly Christian, breathing the spirit of apostolic charity, makes the Bible its only rule of faith, and Christian character its only test of fellowship. What is the action of the church regarding private judgment, which holds some opinion not generally accepted by the membership? If it is merely opinion, if private judgment is really private, if it is a question of belief in the retreat of an earnest christian's soul, what has the local church to do with that? The brother has listened to truth as it has come to him. Perhaps like Apollos he may in time learn the way of God more perfectly. But if he be truly Christian, if he respects in others what he requires for himself, in the Christian Church Christ has set an open door which no man shall shut.

But suppose again that private judgment is not private; suppose it to be heedless of others, demanding all rights and granting none; suppose it to be noisy, quarrelsome, ferocious and inclined to force its idiosyncracies in season and out of season; at once in such case the question is taken out from the simple investigation of private judgment to the larger question of the peace and possibly of the existence of the church. No one doubts the right of the brother to his convictions, but the church will ask itself earnestly whether a quarrelsome and pugnacious disposition is consistent with Christian character, and further, if the peace of the church will not be promoted by permitting him to ventilate his bellicose peculiarities elsewhere. Is not the life more than meat, the body more than raiment, the whole church more than a single man? Is it profitable to set the house on fire so that a stranger may warm his fingers? He cannot ask it. Should he ask it he should expect refusal, and cannot murmur so long as it is courteous, that it is inflexibly firm.

This, then, is the position of the Christian Church in the interpretation of Scripture; declaring always that private judgment is the right and duty of every believer; expecting in consequence that its membership will exhibit diversities of opinion, but trusting always, while the spirit of the Master is cherished, and while brethren obey God rather than man, speaking what seems to them truth in love, that all will "grow up into Him in all things which is the head, even Christ."

www.ingramcontent.com/pod-product-compliance
Lightning Source LLC
Chambersburg PA
CBHW021938160426
43195CB00011B/1135